A Notable Woman: And Other Sketches

Millicent Erskine Wemyss

A NOTABLE WOMAN

And Other Sketches

BY

MILLICENT ERSKINE WEMYSS

EDEN, REMINGTON & CO
LONDON AND SYDNEY.

1893.

PREFACE

To write a short memoir of the ' Princesse des
Ursins' has proved a somewhat more difficult
task than I anticipated. Her life is so entangled in the threads of those who made the
history of the time, that to keep it within
reasonable bounds has been, at any rate for a
tyro, a troublesome achievement. Much that is
interesting—treating of her dealings with the
young King and Queen of Spain, during the trying period of the invasion of their country by the
allied armies—had to be curtailed, while her
relations with both of the Cardinals Bouillon
and Pontocarrero, contained many an element
both of instruction and amusement, and might
have imparted wrinkles to many an accomplished diplomatist.

I do not think her career is so well known to
the general public as her audacious actions and

boundless temerity might lead one to expect
but it is one that is at any rate curiously de-
scriptive of the times, and eminently suggestive
of the political power that could be openly
wielded by a lay woman—if I may be allowed
the term—in the seventeenth century; and I
would say here, that my narrative claims to be
in no way either complete or exhaustive.

I cannot help relating here a trifling incident
that has taken place since this book had the
word 'Finis' written on its last page.

A roving disposition, and no special reason to
prevent its gratification, induced me lately to
visit the old historic châteaux in Tourraine.

Descending at Tours, I established myself in
the centre of their neighbourhood, and the day
after my arrival I went by train to Lemboise,
and there passed some time in examining and
enjoying one of the most stirring and stimulat-
ing localities it is possible to imagine or describe.
Not that Amboise professes greater attraction
than her sister castles, but it was the first I had
visited, and therefore it struck me with all the
fascinating force of novelty.

When I descended into the little town, over
which the castle hangs, I entered the small
calèche that was awaiting me at the foot of the

hill, and drove off in the direction of Cheuon-
ceau, which place I was to visit before returning
to my quarters, at Tours. While crossing, on
this bright and breezy morning, that portion of
the vast and sparkling plain that lies between
the two places, all the country glowing in the
shining sun, I observed in the distance, and at
the very edge of the small forest of Amboise,
an obtrusive column some 150 feet in height.
A column is, of course, distinctive from every
other architectural object. Its simple existence
proclaims a desire to attract attention, to announce some action achieved, to promulgate
some important fact, and I stopped the carriage
and inquired of the driver its signification and
import.

'C'est,' replied he, 'la Colonne de Chauteloup,' and the story of the Princesse des Ursins,
which had interested me for so long, and occupied me too, and that was even now preparing
for publication, reverted to my mind with a
flash of interest and satisfaction only known to
those who unexpectedly come upon an incident
connected with their searchings and investi-
gations. Chauteloup, I remembered, was the
name of the locality that had been selected by
the Princess for the creation of the palace

where she hoped and intended to rule and establish herself as a reigning sovereign, and at Chauteloup d'Aubigny at her hasty, imprudent and ill-advised instigation had raised a magnificent pile on which, and its decoration, he had expended vast sums.

But she had been unable to bend the wills of the European potentates to her own—the peace of Europe was not to be risked for the aggrandisement of Mme. des Ursins, and here, on the very spot where the column was erected, her palace was demolished—her hopes scattered.

The Château was purchased after d'Aubigny's death by the Duc de Choiseul, by him it was sold to the Duc de Penthièvre who raised the column as a monument of gratitude for the kindness of his friends and neighbours towards him during the Revolution.

So says a local guide book, somewhat obscure in its statements as to this last act of grace. But, in any case, the column or pagoda remains, announcing to all who may interest themselves in the matter that here it was that the Princess, knowing no doubt and no fear, vainly gave expression to her pride and her vanity, her presumption and her folly, and thus the column by the cruel irony of fate perpetuates and proclaims her ruin and her fall.

I have only now to express my thanks to Mr Blackwood, and to the Editor of *Temple Bar*, for their courteous permission to reprint the two sketches, 'Paul Jones' and 'Lord George Gordon,' from their respective magazines.— 'André' now appears for the first time.

M. E. W.

Tours, *March* 1893.

CONTENTS

A NOTABLE WOMAN

PART I

CHAPTER I

THE records of the seventeenth and eighteenth centuries display an imposing list of the names of remarkable and sagacious women, who, in that brilliant and splendid age, turned their intellectual and social advantages to account in the political world, and by their tact and acumen more than once changed the course of history. Foremost amongst these adventurous stateswomen, stands the Princesse des Ursins (Orsini), whose tentative and enterprising career forms a study of much interest, swayed as it was by personal ambition, boundless as unscrupulous. Marie Anne de la Tremouille belonged, as her name betokens, to one of the noblest and most ancient families of France, of which her father was the head and representative. He became Duc de Noirmoustier, and took a prominent part in the wars

A

of the Fronde. Biographers differ as to the exact
date of his daughter's birth, but it was probably
about the year 1641. In 1659 her hand was bestowed on Adrien Blaize de Talleyrand, Prince de
Chalais, and she took her place in the highest
ranks of society. She appears to have experienced
happiness and contentment during their union, but
it was of short duration. It was at the time when
the madness for duelling prevailed in France.
Strenuous efforts were being made to check the
custom, 'by which,' says a historian in his *Life of
Henri Quatre*, 'more blood was shed in times of
peace than ever had been spilt in battle.' Her
few last kings had issued stern and relentless edicts
against the practice, while Louis the Fourteenth,
subsequently, reorganised and extended the powers
of the Court of Honour, which, instituted and in-
stalled by Charles IX., had authority to adjudicate
in cases where challenges had been provoked and accepted, and later on, Louis awarded death, and the
forfeiture of honours, rank and estate, to all who
accepted or sent one. Louis' edict had not appeared
when young de Chalais became embroiled in a quarrel
which resulted in the death of the young Duc de
Beauvilliers in 1663. De Chalais had been one of the
'champions' and the law that Richelieu had enforced
in the case of the famous Maréchale de Luxembourg
was in full vigour. The penalties were terrible, and
the enforcement of them unrelenting and pitiless, so
he fled from the disastrous consequences. It was in

Spain, then, that the young Prince took refuge from the retribution that would but too surely follow should he fall into the avenging hands of his sovereign's agents. His wife followed him thither, and it was agreed that their own country being now an impossible domicile, they would make Rome their dwelling-place. With these views, the Princesse de Chalais, leaving her husband in Spain, preceded him to Rome to make the necessary arrangements for their establishment in that city as befitted persons of their rank and importance. A palace was therefore acquired by her, and all preparations made, when, on the eve of the day that she expected to welcome her husband, the overwhelming news of his sudden death reached her (1670). We have no means of learning whether he died by accident or illness ; we have only the fact as stated. Neither are we told whether the misfortune greatly afflicted her. Already everyone of importance, political and social, had rallied round the princess, whose noble birth and distinguished personality had promised to Roman society an acquisition of no small importance and magnificence.

In time a Grandee of Spain and Magnate of Rome offered her his hand. Flavio dei Orsini duca di Bracciano's alliance was a desirable one, and it is probable that the untimely death of the young Prince de Chalais had removed the ban from his widow, for we learn that the court of France signified its approval of the match, and sent the bridegroom, as a mark of distinction and esteem, the order of St Esprit, in 1675.

The Princesse de Chalais, ambitious to improve her
even now high position, burning to free herself from
the shackles that she felt to be oppressive in her
widowed state, thirsting for distinction, for riches, and,
if possible, for action, accepted the offer, and became
Duchesse de Bracciano. She was at this time beautiful, brilliant and sparkling with intelligence and
charm. In the early part of her life in Rome she
had allied herself in intimate friendship with the
Cardinals Bouillon and d'Estrées, who watched the
interests of the French Court at that of the Holy
Father. The Princesse de Chalais had little fortune
and no children. She had much ambition, and so the
Cardinals, recognising her powers and possible influence, induced her to ally herself to Bracciano, who,
never at any time very strong-minded, was persuaded
by them that he was in love with her. He had been
married before, but had had no children, and the new
Duchess, nothing loth to take so high a position,
and with the assurance of a brilliant future to be
carved out by herself, transferred herself to the palace
of Orsini, and became the centre and sovereign ruler
of a species of Court in which all that was distinguished, all that was noble, all that was famous,
gathered itself around her. She is described as being
at this time (1673) somewhat above middle height,
with a magnificent figure, and with *l'air noble*, her
carriage dignified, and all her movements graceful and
natural, her manner gentle and soft, and herself
possessed with a desire of pleasing all. It was im-

possible, says St Simon, not to be agreeably affected
by her presence, and her conversation charmed as
much as did her manner and person. Singularly well
informed and profoundly courteous, she knew how to
apportion her civilities with judgment, vastly ambitious to have, to hold and to govern, she was an
absolute master of *finesse*. Proud, resolute and determined, she achieved her ends without much regard
to the means employed,—good-natured withal,—but
wishing for and doing nothing by halves, a warm friend
and a bitter, implacable foe, such was the Duchess of
Bracciano when she first began her career in Rome.
The family of Bracciano were the head and leaders
of the Roman aristocracy, who bowed themselves down
before the Pope with unequivocal submissiveness and
veneration. Many a cardinal had been drawn by the
different pontiffs from this wealthy source, and thus it
was that the Duke, the chief of this highly important
'Bund,' became very angrily opposed to the decided
and uncompromising views of his headstrong and
resolute wife. Versailles interests and Versailles influence guided her in all her actions and words, and
to the Jesuits she cherished a strong repugnance.
Bracciano's wealth was great, but, notwithstanding
this fact, she tried his resources deeply, and as time
advanced, her wit, brilliancy, political acumen and
haughty self-esteem, bore down his feebler spirit, and
their domestic relations became strained and inhar-
monious. Although his nature was less overbearing
than his wife's, he rebelled against her arrogant

dominion, and her extravagant luxury and enormous expenditure became a serious point of dispute between them. Not only this, but their sympathies—especially political—were widely at variance, and the quarrels between Pope Innocent XI. and Louis XIV. were of so pronounced and serious a character, that it was inevitable they should fan the flame. The French monarch, to whom the Princess pledged her allegiance with obstinate enthusiasm, was in constant antagonism with the Pontiff, and this was the cause of a continuous coldness between husband and wife, for the Bracciano family was nothing if not sacerdotal.

Since the early days of the fifteenth century, when the hand of the young daughter of the princely house of Orsini had been bestowed on Lorenzo the Magnificent—that great and illustrious scion of the house of Medici, by whom she became the mother of the famous Pontiff, Leo X.—the Orsini family had always been accounted as strongly bound to the Holy See. Innocent had unhesitatingly condemned Louis' actions in many matters. Himself proud and masterful, he was accustomed to be obeyed and revered in virtue of his holy office, and Louis' ineffable self-glorification and hauteur irritated him past endurance. Louis, on his part, entirely unaccustomed to remonstrance, let alone reproof or condemnation, offered the Holy Father every affront to which a Pope could be subjected, without taking the serious step of breaking off all communication with him. One of the points of dispute that was most hotly contested between the

sovereign Pontiff and the angry monarch was in the
matter of the ambassadors.   For a long time an abuse
had existed, which, like all others, there was great
difficulty in arresting ; but it *was* an abuse, and as
such was resented by Innocent, while all Catholic
kings piqued themselves on the privilege.   It was
this—all ambassadors claimed the rights of '*asile*' and
'*franchise*,' not only over their own immediate dwelling, but over so large an area of ground, that practically half the city was used as an asylum and a
retreat for crime; and besides this, all entering its
precincts, under the shield of the ambassadors' name,
were remitted from taxation, which, considering the
large number who abused the licence, was highly.
detrimental to commerce.   The Pope gained the consent to the remission of this abuse from Spain, Poland
and England, but Louis haughtily refused, and when
informed of the consent of the other sovereigns, replied ' that he had never been in the habit of following
the example of anyone, and, indeed, that he conceived
that he himself was the one to take the initiative.'
Not content with these arrogant words, he sent his
ambassador to Rome for the mere sake of defying the
Pontiff, whose authority he resented, and whose attitude had so excited his anger, and the Marquis de
Lavardin entered the Holy City in the teeth of Innocent's express commands, escorted by 400 guards,
400 volunteer officers, and 200 men in livery.   He
took possession of the ambassadorial palace, of the
disputed ground, and of the church of St Louis, plac-

ing sentries around as in time of war. The Pope's
position under such circumstances was, of course, exceptional, for while all crowned heads resented the
superiority he assumed, he could yet never retaliate
with force of arms. His soldiers might not fight.
So, all that poor Innocent could do was to excom-
municate them all, and this he did most vigorously.
At that moment, d'Estrées presided over French affairs
at Rome, and being compelled, under the adverse circumstances, to have many interviews with Lavardin,
he could not, according to all the iron rules of popish
pride and etiquette, be permitted to enjoy an audience
of the Pontiff without first receiving absolution. In
vain did d'Estrées struggle and expostulate ; Innocent
did and would absolve him of sins of which he did *not*
repent, and from which he had no desire to be cleansed,
and in the prosecution of which he had every intention of persisting. This, however, was only one of
many disputes of greater moment, perhaps, but of
less picturesque effect. At last, after a bitter quarrel
concerning the bestowal of the bishopric of Cologne,
Louis deprived Innocent XI. of Avignon, and a
quarrel ensued with nearly all the princes of Europe,
who afterwards united against him.

It was probably to escape from the irksomeness of
her relations with her husband—for there was never
any open hostility between them,—as well as for the
sake of ingratiating herself with the French Court,
that twice in the course of her married life of twenty-
three years the Duchess of Bracciano took refuge

from its asperities under the hospitable roof of her
friend and relative, the Maréchale de Noailles. During her absence, probably to counterbalance his wife's
defiance of his wishes and tenets, Bracciano, having
no child of his own to inherit his wealth and his
name, and perhaps also to make compensation to
Innocent XI. for her inimical and intractable demeanour, adopted, as his successor, Don Livio Odescalchi,
the Pontiff's nephew.

It was in the course of her second visit, which
lasted five years, that Louis XIV. began to tread the
thorny path of adversity. Hitherto unshaken in his
overweening pride and confidence in his own power
and authority, and troubled by no disquieting doubts
regarding their ultimate success and perpetual stability, his attitude towards nearly all the princes
and potentates of European states, was inconceivably
haughty and arrogant. The Augsburg Alliance was
formed by these injured and aggrieved princes in
1688, to oppose the intolerable aggression of France.
There was hardly any prince that was not tingling
with resentment and anger. Louis had seized on
Strasburg in 1681, and thus opened himself up a new
way to Germany. He had invaded the Palatinate
to enforce a worthless claim made by his sister-in-
law, although it had been rejected by the Imperial
Courts; and as the army was powerless to hold Strasburg, it had ravaged the country, destroying towns
and crops, and laying it waste. The Dutch, indeed,
rather than submit to the invader, had resorted to

the desperate expedient of destroying the dykes
and sea-walls that protected their low-lying country
from the inroads of their less cruel and less humiliating enemy—the ocean ;—an act that so amazed
Louis by its desperate heroism and magnificent
resolution, that his army retreated. In William of
Orange he had a dangerous and determined foe, and
their mutual antipathy was not diminished by a
former incident that we may be sure was always
present in their dealings with each other. Some,
years before, when William was on a visit to
Versailles, Louis had offered him the hand of one of
his illegitimate daughters, Mdlle. de Blois. 'The
Princes of Orange,' replied William haughtily, 'are
not in the habit of marrying kings' bastards, but
their legitimate offspring'—a reply that Louis never
forgot or forgave, probably because it was so well
merited. By the revocation of the Edict of Nantes,
Louis did himself, in 1685, an injury that perhaps
was more the cause of his décadence than even his
other acts of arrogance and folly ; for a bitter, revo-
lutionary and incensed spirit spread itself amongst
a large portion of the people, and a chronic feeling
of rebellion was roused in the Cevennes, the principal
home of the injured Protestants. In 1692, the naval
defeat of La Hogue was a serious blow to his
prestige; Namur was wrested from him by the
avenging William in 1694, and the Peace of Ryswick
was forced upon the mortified King, unused to
coercion, compulsion, or even contradiction.

In spite of his obstinate and haughty aggressions,
it is certain that at the early period of Louis' life all
his intentions were good, all his impulses generous,
all his feelings noble. Still, no one inheriting the
infirmities of vain and weak human nature, born in
the purple, bred in the blinding light of adulation,
praise and obsequious flattery, and surrounded by
courtiers worshipping at his shrine, can survive
the process without demoralisation, and although
Mazarin directed and ordered his establishment, the
cardinal took little heed of him else. He was left
entirely in the hands of women for long after the
time that masculine authority and instruction were
necessary. Nominally, he had a tutor and a governor,
actually a nurse and a lady-in-waiting. An *enfant
d'honneur* was placed about his person when quite a
little boy, and it is droll to read of the formal installation of the child, at which ceremony several other
infants of tender years and noble birth assisted.
Madame de Salle, the Queen's *femme de chambre* (probably invested with a more important charge than the
name implies), received them at the head of the stairs
—some especially accomplished babies beating the
drums,—colours flying, lances in hand, the *hausse-col*
lying on her own well-cut and starched handkerchief,
which was tied in the strictest military form—a man's
hat, with feathers, on her head, and a sword hanging by
her side. To every child of this baby regiment Louis
gave a musket, which the recipient accepted, hand
on hat, without uncovering—this being 'regulation.'

Madame de Salle kissed them all when parade was
over, blessed them piously, gave the order for the
exercise to be practised that day, and dismissed the
veteran force with another kiss, which sounds more
maternal than military.

Louis disliked Mazarin cordially. He made the
grave error of treating the young King with carelessness and indifference. Brought up by the cardinal and his mother in profound ignorance of all
that it most concerned a king to know, at the age
of twenty-two he was still in bondage when the
cardinal died. While yet a lad of eighteen his
dawning intelligence found an eager pleasure in de-
vouring poetry and romances, but he had received
neither education nor enlightenment from any com-
petent instructor or adviser, and had, indeed, been
cruelly and even wickedly neglected. It was
Mazarin's desire that he *should* be ignorant. His
sapient perspicuity had discerned qualities in the
crude and unformed character of Louis, that he
probably feared might some day develop themselves
to his own detriment. 'There is enough stuff in him,'
said the far-seeing cardinal, 'to make four kings and
one honest man.' But alas! the process of king-mak-
ing marred the construction of the honest man. That
Louis was a king in the true sense of the word, however, may be seen in a collection of his works, published
in 1806, and of whose authenticity we may be assured,
since St Beuve, that accomplished historian and keen-
eyed critic, accepts them as genuine. 'They are,'

says he, 'veritable memoirs of his reign, written for the perusal of his son.' Louis cultivated in his Court such extraordinary magnificence, that he became the cynosure of the whole civilised world. His splendour was apparent in his least actions, and as life opened by degrees before his observant eyes he felt stirring within him the ambition to eclipse in glory and renown all that had gone before in history. Naturally gracious and kind-hearted—the first element necessary for really good manners—Louis added to the proud yet gentle ways of his mother, a dignity of demeanour, a courtesy of speech, and a brilliancy of conversation all his own. But we must not digress further, but return to the text of our story.

Unable to avoid or evade the conditions of Ryswick, Louis' hope of regeneration now lay in the chances of acquisition of the throne of Spain. The power and influence of that country which had been almost without limit or precedent in the sixteenth century, had declined, to an extent almost incredible, in so short a time, and during the reigns of the three last kings, Philippes the Third and Fourth, and the present occupant of the throne, Charles the Second, the last male heir of the Austrian line. Entirely destitute of health, moral or physical; of character good or evil; this feeble monarch still possessed one redeeming point in his otherwise insignificant and inane character. It was a quality of little use to anyone, and only caused himself pitable suffer-

ing, for he was powerless to redeem it—it was the
knowledge of his own incompetence.

Louis XIV. and the Emperor Leopold were related
to Charles in the same degree. Both descended in
the female line from Philippe III., but Louis was the
son of the eldest sister, so that Louis' children had
the advantage over Leopold's. They had also married two half-sisters, both of whom were daughters
of Philippe IV. Louis' wife was descended from
Philippe III., while Leopold's wife was not. Louis,
on his marriage with the Infanta Marie Therese, had
renounced all ultimate claims to the Spanish crown.
This did not prevent his straining every nerve to
obtain possession of the coveted sovereignty which
it was in the power of the weakling King to will and
devise. Charles II. had been twice married, and at
this juncture his failing health had already given an
impetus to the greedy ambitions of his possible heirs.
He had just enough understanding to appreciate the
horrors of the fact that all the European wolves were
howling round him, thirsting for his death and their
own inheritance,—just enough conscience to desire to
act justly, just enough intellect to realise that his will
would settle an affair of vast and world-wide importance. So he vacillated, hesitated, debated—suffered,
of course—and made fresh wills as often as a fresh
counsellor entreated. Only thirty-nine at the time
of his death, he had all the appearance, constitution
and infirmities of an aged man. The succession
would have been a difficult matter to arbitrate, even

had he been one full of capacities and vigour. Many
were the testaments destroyed by the unhappy monarch,
whose feeble and ebbing life must have been a martyr-
dom the last few months of his reign. It was widely
desired that his decision should be in favour of the
House of Austria. He had made a will propitious to
a Prince of Bavaria, the son of his niece, but in 1698
this child died—probably by poison ; but this question
is foreign to our present subject. Poor Charles' feeble
thread of life nearly snapped when he was once more
subjected to the heartless torments of his persecutors.
Beset on all sides, humiliated and wounded, he felt
there could be no peace for him but in the consumma-
tion so devoutly desired by all. In this terrible crisis
Pontocarrero arrived from Rome. Weak, ignorant, but
possessed by a feeble, half-developed desire to act in the
true interests of Spain, Charles signed what at that
moment he deemed to be the best for his country's weal.

The Duchess of Bracciano had, during her stay with
the Maréchale de Noailles, made the acquaintance of
Torcy, who, deep in the confidence of his royal master,
had the acuteness to see in her a possible assistant in
these ambitious aspirations. She was presented to
Madame Maintenon, then all powerful in her anomal-
ous, but unassailable, position of unacknowledged wife
of Louis XIV., and while Torcy fully appreciated the
resources of her mind, he resolved that she should be
the instrument whereby the desired end should be
attained. He took her into his confidence, he explained his hopes and his fears, and he recommended

her to the Spanish Ambassador at Rome, whither
the declining health of her husband now called her.
Thither she returned, and was fortunate enough to find
Cardinal Pontocarrero, the Archbishop of Toledo, who
had journeyed thither to receive, from the hands of
Innocent XI., a cardinal's hat. He was of high
descent and of considerable power of intellect. A
Castillian by birth, and also by nature, he had always
exercised a certain power over Charles. He was the
first subject in Spain, and made no secret of his
opinion that power, might, majesty and dominion were
his by right, and while he fully intended to influence
the choice of the successor to the throne of Spain, he
was not altogether unwilling it should fall to a scion
of the Royal family of France, provided that family
made it worth his while to achieve this end. His
haughty character inspired many with fear, for his
thirst for power was unquenchable, his resolution in-
domitable, and his means of carrying out his intentions
unscrupulous, and by the exercise of these overwhelming qualities, he commanded respect and obtained submission. Such was the character of the man who,
by the common instinct of his kind, recognised in
the ambitious Duchess a kindred spirit—one whose
connections and influence, both in Rome and Paris,
might be a useful assistant in whatever policy he
might decide upon. But besides all this, her presence
pleased him, her intellect surprised him,—there were
none such in Spain,—and she possessed all the subtle
qualities of the female diplomatist, including the sixth

sense often wanting in the male. So he resolved to learn her weaknesses, to study her opinions and mould them to his own, a resolution which she, on her part, also took with regard to his.

———

CHAPTER II

As early as 1673 the Princesse de Chalais became the object of political intrigue and great interest to those skilled in political arts. At the death of Philippe IV., his widow, Marie Anne of Austria, became Queen Regent for her son, Charles II. Cardinal Nithard, her confessor, was a man of low birth but great talent for intrigue, and he had measured the capacities of the Princesse de Chalais with whom he had lived on terms of friendship, and had resolved, if possible, to annex her services for the benefit of the House of Austria, and to secure and seal them by some overwhelming gift or obligation. Nithard himself, at Philippe's death, became Grand Inquisitor, naturalised himself a Spaniard, and became complete master of the Queen Regent, and absolute director of all Spanish affairs ; to the passionate indignation of all the grandees, who resolved to destroy his power and prestige. Nithard was expelled from Spain by an *émeute* and retired, refusing all compensation from the Queen Regent, who

B

nominated him ambassador to Rome. The mob would
have massacred him, but the Archbishop of Toledo
succeeded in saving his life. 'I entered Spain a penni-
less monk,' said Nithard when the Queen pressed gold
upon him, 'I will depart as I came.' He wrote from
Rome to the Spanish Ambassador of Vienna to urge
the Princess's claims and talents, and to beg him to
press the Emperor to bestow on her the gift and
dignity of a German Principality. The Prince de
Chalais, her husband, had fought gallantly in the interest of Spain, and in the war that had ended in
Portugal declaring her independence; but in spite
of all his representations, the prayer was rejected.
That Madame de Chalais was at this time intriguing
with the two countries is, of course, clear. D'Estrées
was endeavouring to persuade her to end her intimacy
with Nithard, an injunction that she evaded for some
time, playing the two rival aspirants for her patronage
against each other; and when the Emperor finally
declined to yield to Nithard's solicitations, she threw
herself into the arms of France, and in the supposed
interests of that country became in later years both
the servant and master of Spain. The ambition, however, of her life was to became *altesse*, and some
forty years later, as will be seen, she did not hesitate
to endanger the peace of Europe for the gratification
of this desire, influencing Philippe the Fifth to exact,
when the terms for the treaty for Utrecht were being
laid down, the cession to the Elector of Bavaria of the
Spanish Low Countries, in exchange for the loss of the

Germanic Provinces and the confirmation to and endowment of Marie Anne de la Tremouille, Princesse des Ursins, as an independent sovereign.

CHAPTER III

On her return to Rome in 1698 she had resumed her receptions. Her *salon* was thrown open to all sorts and conditions of public men, and distinguished persons flocked thither, while all other reunions, political and otherwise, paled before these in importance and magnificence. She was full of talent, both diplomatic and social, of charm of manner, of art, esprit, dignity, and all united together to produce a marked social success and personal triumph. All the letters written by her at this time to the Maréchale de Noailles teem with the consciousness of ascendency, with the triumph of anticipated victory. 'On y est avec liberté,' she says in one which describes her reunions, 'parceque c'était la coutume et qu'en outre on y pouvait parler à des gens qu'il était difficile de rencontrer ailleurs.' The fame of her *salon*, of her wit and her wisdom, went out to all the Courts of Europe, and the new Pope, on his succession to the Holy See, expressed to her brother the Abbé, afterwards Cardinal de la Tremouille, an ecclesiastic whose talent lay more in the

enjoyment of buffoonery than in that of holiness—
the desire he had to make her personal acquaintance,
adding that he would gladly ask her advice on many
things, and that he was confident that her opinion was
of greater value than that of all his cardinals put together. The Duchess of Bracciano did not content
herself with the society of members of the highest
grade in the social scale, for wherever she found ability,
talent, energy and goodwill, she availed herself of them,
and often went far afield in pursuit of them. She informed herself of the capabilities and proclivities, of the
character and actions of all who could be turned to
the smallest political use.

But in the midst of her campaign her husband
died. He was an inferior and feeble being as we
have before intimated, and we can easily understand
that he had been overwhelmed by his wife's superiority and influence. Pontocarrero, who was the
friend of both, had negotiated a reconciliation between them, and not only did he effect this, but to such
good purpose, that the Duke left his widow the whole
of his fortune, to the indignant dismay of Don Livio
Odescalchi. A long and complicated litigation ensued, the Duchess defending her rights with vigour
from the young pretender's onslaughts, while he,
on his side, had good cause for complaint when we
consider the customs of the times, for adopted
sons had nearly as good a claim to the rights
of relationship as if they were really of the same
flesh and blood as their adopted fathers. Don

Livio produced papers that seemed to prove his case,
but as most of them were forgeries which invali-
dated the rest, the process threatened to be endless.
Louis himself interposed in favour of one who was in
the midst of important diplomatic negotiations on
his behalf. Don Livio unblushingly acknowledged the
forgeries and gave up the forged papers, but none
the less did he pursue the case. The Duke had died
deeply in debt, but what Don Livio coveted more than
the wealth was the title, while the Tribunal, in face of
the importance of both of the contending parties
knew not how to decide, justice and equity being
entirely subordinate elements in the case. The
Duchess possessed estates, houses, lands, and very
little cash, so, to compromise matters, it was suggested
that in return for the duchy which should then be delivered to Don Livio, a large sum of money, for he
was already a rich man, should be paid by him for its
rights. At this juncture the Pope, hoping to soothe
matters and appease the Duchess's wrath, desirous of
propitiating both parties, suceeded in making enemies
of each. He suggested, as a softening alternative, that
his nephew should become a cardinal, thus opening
up to that irritated and angry litigant a perspective of
conditional Roman purple, at least as brilliant as his
alternative aspirations. But the Duchess viewed the
case differently. The sum of money that had been
suggested was a modification of circumstances she was
not slow to appreciate, and was loth to surrender. The
name of Bracciano did not sound so musical in her

ear as in the Pontiff's nephew's, and she was quite contented to assume the second title of her husband's
family.   Her own debts were considerable, her luxury,
her entertainments, her magnificences having cost enormous sums.   To Don Livio, however, the cardinal
alternative was the more seductive of the two.   In the
very middle of the discussions and negotiations, of the
representations and contentions, death claimed the
temporising Pope, and thus involuntarily settled the
question in favour of the Duchess of Bracciano.   Don
Livio bitterly regretted this conclusion, but he was
compelled to accept the title of Bracciano and hand
her over two millions of ducats, having thus lost
the chance of the cardinal's hat.   From this moment
the Duchess assumed the second title of her late husband's family, and turning the name of Orsini into its
French equivalent, was for all time thereafter, known
as the Princesse des Ursins.   Large as was the sum
she received, nine-tenths of it were needed for the
discharge of her debts, and she applied to Louis, who
had already granted her a pension to direct the
Spanish negotiation, to supplement her income, for
she did not view a decrease of luxury and state with
equanimity.

The Princess and Pontocarrero were, in the course
of all these transactions and manœuvrings, brought
still nearer together.   His influence over her deceased
husband, resulting in so satisfactory a conclusion, had
done much towards atoning for the long discontent
and vexation of spirit from which she had suffered

during the period of her marriage, and a brilliant
career seemed to be forming itself out of the mass of
incoherent possibilities that lay now before her. She
owed him an enormous debt of gratitude, which was
to be enormously increased, and like all, or most of such
burdens, to be eventually cast down and ignored. She
recognised the fact that Austria would, in all human
and diplomatic probability, win the race, unless by
some special act of skill and adroitness their own cause
could be strengthened. She therefore took the reins
into her own persuasive hands, and by subtle flattery
and gentle coercion, by artful words and skilful wiles,
assuring him at the same time that the highest benefits
would accrue to him personally by the transaction,
so dexterously manipulated his greed and his vanity,
his pride and his prejudices, that only a few days before Charles II.'s death Pontocarrero arrived at Madrid,
confident that an interview with the dying monarch
was all that was needful to direct the succession into
the line that he desired. The result proved that he
did not miscalculate his powers, for although the King
had quite recently made a will in favour of the Archduke Charles, Leopold's son, he was no sooner attacked by Pontocarrero than he was persuaded, by the
arguments and wiles of that crafty priest, to destroy
the document and execute another in favour of the
Duc d'Anjou. Fortunately for Louis, Charles died
almost immediately afterwards, or else he would certainly have changed what might have been, by courtesy,
called his mind as often as he was required to do so,

by the interested agents of greedy heirs. Thus was
Madame des Ursins' first diplomatic effort brilliantly
and eminently successful. Louis increased her pension and she was launched into the diplomatic service,
an official, though secret, member of that enticing
profession.

And, indeed, it was in the face of great difficulties,
and by dint of great efforts, that Madame des Ursins
had obtained her object, for the legitimate ambassador
from France was at this time Cardinal Bouillon, her
quondam friend and intimate. His appointment in
1698 had been a highly injudicious one, for he was,
at the best of times, but an imperfect Frenchman.
German in sympathies and feelings, he was half a
German by birth, a cousin of William of Orange, and
of several German princes, and never took the trouble
at any time to conceal his preferences for his mother's
country. The object of his ambition was to become
Prince Archbishop of Liége, by which means the
title and rank of *altesse* would have become his by
right, and to the attainment of which honour he
vied with Madame des Ursins in the vehemence of
his desire. In 1694 the See had become vacant,
and nothing doubting but that his request would be
granted, he had besought Louis and Innocent XI. to
bestow it upon him. To his irrepressible mortification,
it had been refused. But, besides this, he had another
grievance against Louis, of what he deemed great
magnitude, which fanned his fury and drove him to
a species of revenge as foolish as insolent. In Auvergne

there were two sorts of estates held by a peculiar tenure, the one called the County of Auvergne, and the other the Dauphiné ; these two had always hitherto been possessed by one of the princes of the blood royal, and themselves conferred upon their possessor the dignity of *altesse.* He therefore offered a large sum to the Dauphin for the Dauphiné, but when the King heard of the transaction, he forbade its completion. So exasperated was Bouillon at this decision that he had the folly to vent his disappointment and rage in a satire of so insolent a nature that he was banished from the Court. But Louis, never rancorous or ill-natured, especially in matters personal, recalled him, and after the Peace of Ryswick appointed him ambassador to Rome, where he established himself in great pomp and splendour in 1699.

The impending vacancy of the Spanish throne at this time filled the minds of all, but in spite of his official position, Bouillon ignored all the instructions which had been given him by his master, and secretly devoted himself to the interests of the Austrian candidate. He had conceived a violent hatred to Madame de Bracciano, or Madame des Ursins, as she had now become, suspecting her of having used her interest five years before to deprive him of the object of his ambition, and although she made every effort to induce him to assist her, he refused to come to any understanding on the subject with her. He employed one Abbé de Vauban to spy upon her, and to obtain every possible

information concerning her efforts, actions, sayings and
doings, and shortly after the Duke of Bracciano died
he pursued a course of petty and spiteful actions that
were as mean as they were annoying. Pushing to its
extreme a point of etiquette which had lately been
honoured by the breach rather than by the observance,
he, immediately on the death of her husband, presented
himself to the widowed Duchess, and persisted in
exacting the performance of the old Roman custom
of dining at her table and in her company. Etiquette
had all her life wearied Madame de Bracciano—she
was accustomed to follow in all ways the dictates of
her own humour—French ways were less formal than
Roman customs; she had never been used to be
gênée; the peculiar charm of her *salon* and of her
surroundings was freedom from ceremony, and the
requisition of the obtrusive cardinal filled her with
anger. She flatly refused, but still he insisted, and
that in a tone both offensive and insolent, and the
Duchess therefore caused him to be served in the
ante-chamber of her apartment, and alone—a slight he
never forgave. More than this. Besides being French
Ambassador, he was the Sous-Doyen of the Sacred
College. It was the custom that the death of so high
and important a noble as the Duke of Bracciano
should be followed by various forms and ceremonies
which involved what were regarded as privileges.
Madame de Bracciano, in accordance with that vouch-
safed to the eldest scions of the house, hung her palace
with violet, and the cardinal immediately ordained

and exacted that it should be hung with black. After this the rupture became complete, but as once before, Bouillon's anger and petty spite outran his discretion. It was now war to the knife between the violent and virulent cardinal and the subtle and resolute Duchess, who wielded her pen with as much dexterity and success as did the most able and valiant warrior his sword. She roundly and truthfully informed those at head-quarters that Bouillon was Austrian in sympathies and at heart a traitor to the French cause. Moreover, she convinced the Maréchale de Noailles of the truth of what she said. It was the death-blow to his influence, for at that time Madame de Noailles was all in all with Madame de Maintenon, and Bouillon had cause to rue his spite and his folly, the acrimony of his words and the impetuosity of his temper. He received his recall, and the Prince de Monaco was named his successor. Like many another of his sort, Bouillon was entirely unprepared for so condign a punishment—for so positive a recognition of the actual state of affairs.—He worked day and night to get the sentence revoked, to ruin his successor, to get the nomination rescinded, but Madame de Bracciano was equal to the occasion. All his insinuations and falsehoods were dissipated by her. She protected Monaco, affirmed that he was the *protégé* of the Noailles—of the King,—that he was *her* friend, how then could he be otherwise than devoted to France? So judiciously did she act, so wisely did she reason, so unhesitating was her demeanour, that before long all Bouillon's deceptions were defeated.

On November 1st, 1700, Charles II. died, and the Duc d'Anjou the Dauphin's second son and Louis' grandson, was shortly after proclaimed King of Spain by the right of the deceased King's will, while the Princesse des Ursins, her mission accomplished, her merits recognised, proud, successful and triumphant, rested from her labours and began to think of the future.

When Philippe V. succeeded to the Spanish throne the condition of Spain was one of such debasement and degradation as it seems difficult to realise. The extraordinary prosperity, wealth and advancement of civilisation that had marked the glorious reigns of Ferdinand and Isabella, the Emperor Charles the Fifth, and Philippe the Second had not only crumbled away to the very earth, but her subsequent rulers had, during the last sixty years, been so steeped in superstition, inertness, torpor and incapacity, that the very glory of the past days served but to show up more clearly the corruption and abjectness of her present condition, the result of their discreditable reigns. No class, save the ecclesiastical one, flourished. The army and navy lacked commanders, commerce had practically ceased to exist, the arts and sciences had dwindled away, education there was none, knowledge and understanding there were none,—the country was doomed, diseased,—stricken.—We are not attempting to write a history of Spain, so we can only touch

on these matters to let a little light in upon our
subject.

The Spaniards accepted their foreign king half
jealously and half reluctantly, but still we imagine
with something of curiosity and of hope that a better
development might follow. The nobles were to the
full as ignorant, as uneducated, as deteriorated and as
superstitious as all the rest of the nation, and the
advent of the foreign rule was probably looked upon
as a chance of better things to come, for when matters
get to so low an ebb, almost any change must be for
the better. There were at least a certain number of
Frenchmen in Philippe's train who imparted new
ideas. Nothing of grandeur remained in Spain but
the inflated pride of the grandees. There sole conception of dignity lay in the number of their own
titles, and in the acts of etiquette to which they could
subject the royal family. Even *they* could not but
see how empty and incapable, how flat, stale and
unprofitable were all the sounding brass and tinkling
cymbals indicative of nothing but vanity, that
formed the only foundation of the Spanish Court.
Thus did the young French prince, fresh from magni-
ficient Versailles, and accustomed to the splendour
of such a monarchy, step into the midst of the
desolate ruin of departed greatness, and survey
with a not too intelligent curiosity the nakedness of
the land.

Had thrice as many summers passed over the
boyish and incompetent head of Philippe d'Anjou,

he would still have been incapable to deal with the
task that lay before him—one with which a Richelieu
alone could have grappled.   Judgment, decision, a
strong will, and a natural capacity for governing alone
could have made his efforts even possibly successful.
As it was, besides lacking these qualities, he was of
course absolutely without experience, and as destitute
of any training as he was of natural sagacity.   His
eldest brother, the Duc de Bourgogne, the eventual
heir to the French throne, violent in temper, arrogant
in demeanour, and subject to the most furious and
ungovernable fits of temper, had quelled his brother's
spirit, and by his tyranny had finished by making him
a victim and a slave.   When the young King passed
from his own country to that of his adoption, he being
then seventeen years old, he was escorted and accompanied by certain courtiers and advisers, selected by
Louis, who were of course instructed to report fully
.to himself.   In spite of the pride and triumph that
swelled in his breast, the French King must have been
troubled by many doubts as to the result of so
enormous a venture, supported by such inadequate
auxiliaries.   It is true that he intended practically to
be himself King of Spain, but he was too experienced
a statesman and politician not to recognise the
perils that must accrue through the distance from
the scene of action, although it is possible that
he preferred the dangers of passive, if blunder-
ing, obedience to those of experienced opposition.
Philippe had been brought up in the greatest awe

of his grandfather, and, indeed, up to the time of his accession, his life had been one constant habit of nervous submission to the wills and caprices of others. The transition could not but have been trying in the extreme. For the first time in his life, Louis had approached his grandson, now suddenly elevated to regal rank, in the sense of companionship and equality. This sort of occasion was his stalking horse. The magnificent monarch was an adept in suiting his sonorous admonitions to the occasion, and his stilted words to the public ear; 'Pour nous,' said he, pompously and epigrammatically, when he took leave of his grandson, 'pour nous les Pyrénées n'existent plus,' and doubtless, he spoke as he hoped. But those gigantic mountains were not to be removed by an epigram, whatever they might have been by faith, and they reared their majestic heights in upstanding and direct contradiction of his assertion. Time and space had not then been conquered by science, and telegraphs did not exist to warn, to threaten and command. Possibly, had Philippe had strength of will and purpose and some force of character he might (behind the mountains) have become an independent sovereign and reigned supreme, but he remained a ductile material in Louis' cunning hands until another artist possessed herself of the plastic clay and moulded it as she would.

CHAPTER IV

No sooner had Louis despatched his grandson to take
his place on the Spanish throne, than he took steps
to ensure him a companion in the shape of a wife;
and the Duchess of Burgundy's sister (the daughter
of the Duc of Savoy) being disengaged—well, she
was but thirteen years old—and Louis being more
fondly devoted to his grandson's wife than to any
other person, resolved that she should become
Queen of Spain, and on the 11th September 1701,
a marriage by proxy was solemnised at Turin between Philippe V. and Louise Marie of Savoy. Meantime Madame des Ursins watched the march of events
from Rome, with anxious eyes, and no sooner was
the question of the marriage broached than she cast
about to see in what manner she could ally herself
with the new Court. The possibilities appertaining to
her own position soon developed themselves in her
fructifying mind, and she approached the Pope and
obtained his sympathies and concurrence in her projects, as well as those of the Spanish Ambassador at
Rome. The *fiancée* was but a child, and it was
certain that a lady of high rank and intelligence would
be required to direct her steps, her household, and
her conduct. She wrote to Madame de Noailles, who
had been the original source of her acquaintance with
Madame de Maintenon, setting forth her own quali-

fications and fitness for the post, and requested her
to lay the matter before Louis. She flaunted her
own political power and talents, and approached her
friend, as all good diplomatists should, by an appeal
to her personal and private interest. The Maréchale
was the anxious and vigilant mother of twenty-one
children, eleven of whom were daughters. 'Procure
me what I desire,' said the Princess, 'and I will marry
for you *une douzaine de vos filles.*' (We may add
here that if she did not carry out her promise in all
its fulness, yet she did requisition some of Philippe's
subjects for the achievement of her large enterprise.)
Not receiving the appointment she coveted as soon
as she hoped for, she wrote again to her friend still
more urgently. 'Only let me attend the young Queen
as far as Madrid,' she said, 'and I will leave her as
soon as she arrives there.' But the crafty old diplomatist knew well that, once attached to the person
of the Queen, she would not be likely to return.
Madame de Maintenon was the close and intimate
friend of Madame de Noailles, and it was through
her influence that Madame des Ursins finally obtained the appointment she so desired. In spite of
all the shrewdness of Madame de Maintenon, she
firmly believed that Madame des Ursins was, or
would become in her new position, her own sub-
sidiary puppet, while the latter continued to make
them all believe that her acceptance of the post was
at least as great an advantage to the French Court
as to herself. On June 21st the Princess writes the

joyful news of her official appointment. She speaks
with much detail of her outfit and necessaries, of the
liveries of her servants, of her carriages and attendants, and of her resolution to have no Italian in-
triguants in her household.   So she quitted Rome
and journeyed to Genoa, St Simon relates, to take
charge of and instruct the little Queen, so childish
and young to be thus separated from her own family
and country, and practically launched into a new
world, in a new position and among a fresh people.
Having been married by proxy, she embarked at
Nice, on the 20th September, for Barcelona, and was
met and congratulated on her marriage by envoys
from the Pope, and even from the German Emperor,
glooming as he was over the Spanish succession.
The King of Spain, not one whit older in his beard-
less boyhood than was his bride in her childish simplicity, left Pontocarrero at Madrid to administer state
affairs in his absence, and made a magnificent progress towards Barcelona to welcome his *fiancée*.
Young as was the little Queen, it is said that she possessed singular judgment for her age, and Madame
des Ursins was much pleased with the promise of
an intelligent and capable pupil.   On the frontier
she was met by a messenger bearing her presents
from the King, and at Figuières, two days' journey
from Barcelona, he himself welcomed her to Spanish
soil.   According to previous arrangement, the whole
of her Savoyard suite left her here, only one or two
ladies-in-waiting on her person remaining.   She cried

bitterly when they took leave of her and rode away,
seeming bewildered and uneasy at the new faces of
the Spanish household who accompanied her bridegroom. He, when some distance off, had eagerly
mounted his horse and galloped to meet her, and
the Princesse des Ursins introduced the two young
creatures to one another. They were at once re-
married with little pomp, and the nuptial banquet,
served immediately after the ceremony, was the
cause of much distress and pain to the little bride.
The dishes had been composed with great efforts at
impartiality, partly *à la Française*, partly *à l'Espagnole*,
but the Spanish ladies were extremely indignant at
the intrusion of the French dishes, and probably still
more so at that of Madame des Ursins. Her appointment to the important post of Camerera-Major was
usually filled by one of the highest born of the Spanish
nobility, so that not only did they deeply resent the
affront of her presence and appointment, but they
displayed their very ill-bred resentment by deliberately
upsetting each dish as they presented it. This they
effected by pretence of its being either too hot to hold
or too big to carry, or by feigning to stumble themselves, and thus letting it fall, each separate dish meeting with the same fate. Everyone, as well as the
dishes was upset—the intention was too palpable for
even the pretence of its being an accident. The King
and Queen had the self-control—astonishing in such
children—to pretend to remark nothing, but when they
were alone poor little Louise Marie cried and sobbed

piteously at an insult so unmistakable. She thought
that she would be exposed all her life to the indignities
of these rude and cruel Spanish ladies. More than
this, her temper was roused, and with more irascibility
than reason she turned her back on Philippe, who
was of course as angry at the occurrence as herself.
Madame des Ursins strove in vain to calm her anger,
and to reconcile the angry bride and the dismayed
bridegroom. Every kind of remonstrance was employed by her—entreaties, prayers, even commands—
but to no purpose, and Philippe soon became as angry
with her as she was with him, and they parted in high
dudgeon each one to their own apartment. The Queen
declared that somehow or other she would contrive to
return to her own country, while those of her followers
that remained remonstrated, and consternation reigned
everywhere. But she only sobbed and cried the more
for her own country and her own people, and she
would not be pacified, nor would she consent to take
up her position as Queen of Spain till the next day.
Then, however, Madame des Ursins found matters
still further complicated by the King persisting in his
attitude of hostility, and he in his turn tossed his head
and refused to see his wife. Although this exhibition
of temper was the result of artless and boyish anger,
rather than artful premeditation, it was the precise
attitude calculated to win the Queen over, for it hurt
her *amour propre* and her vanity. She showed signs
of relenting that were gladly seized upon by Madame
des Ursins, and shortly after the ladies-in-waiting

were reproved for their conduct, the gentlemen in
attendance remonstrated with on their rudeness,
a word of warning was given here, a smile of en-
couragement there, the happy result being ex-
·cuses, apologies, pardons, promises and assurances.
Everyone was forgiven, the King and the Queen
reconciled, and they all left Figuières together the
best of friends.

Several letters written by Madame des Ursins, soon
after her arrival in Madrid, to Madame de Noailles describe the manners and customs of that Court. It is to
be remembered that so far from being a young woman,
she was, according to the least remote date of her supposed birth, at any rate sixty years of age; moreover, she
was not of a very robust constitution, and her account
of her duties are highly surprising and suggestive.
Those of the Camerera-Major, in spite of the supposed
stateliness of the function, seem to have been as
ignoble as strange, and are thus described by the
Princess : ' Dans quel emploi, bon Dieu !' says she to
her friend in Nov. 1701, soon after her entrance on her
onerous duties, 'dans quel emploi m'avez vous mise!
Rest have I none, neither time to give orders to my
secretary. I need not hope to rest after dinner, nor,
indeed, to eat when I am hungry ; I consider myself
fortunate if I am able to eat a hurried meal as I walk,
and if I do happen to sit down I am certain to be called
away. Truly Madame de Maintenon would laugh if
she knew the details of my office. Pray tell her that to
me belongs the honour of undressing the King when

he gets into bed, and of handing him his slippers when
he gets out ; and, if it stopped here, I should not com-
plain, but every night the King enters the Queen's
room, the Duc de Benavente entrusts me with the care
of his majesty's sword, and with other necessaries'
(which the Princess clearly specifies, but which we
will not), 'and with a lamp, which I invariably upset
over my clothes—it is too droll. Never, I am certain,
would the King get up at all, did I not draw back the
curtains, and it would be sacrilege, did anyone but myself enter the room where he and the Queen are in
bed. The other day the lamp went out because I had
spilled the oil. We had only arrived the same night,
and I did not remember the position of the windows,
and I expected every moment to break my nose
against the wall. The King got up, and we were a
quarter of an hour before we found out where we were.
The King is so amazingly pleased with me, that he
sometimes has the great kindness to have me called
two hours before I desire to rise. The Queen enters
into it all, but all the same I have not yet gained the
confidence that was enjoyed by her Piedmontaise
femme-de-chambre. Why I know not, for I serve her
far better, and I am certain they did not wash her
feet, and take off her shoes and stockings as I do.'
Thus the Princesse des Ursins in the first days of her
service in Madrid. But menial as this seems to have
been at this time, she rose to other altitudes later on,
and in whatever terms she may have deemed it
prudent to write to her friends, from the moment

she entered on her charge she took the helm. Two children lay practically in the hollow of her hand to do with, as far as they were concerned, as she would. Philippe, himself, was a lad of naturally good disposition, but he had received the slenderest possible education, was weak, boyish, irresponsible, and indifferent to affairs of state. His young wife was bright, keen, eager and intelligent. Madame des Ursins played on her affections skilfully, instructing and interesting her, the result being an almost passionate affection for one who dealt with her as a loving and devoted mother. Louise Marie had been very carefully brought up, and she understood her position; she had strength of character, and much gentleness, and was capable of the warmest affection. Naturally graceful in appearance and manner, she also displayed later on, in very trying circumstances, both courage and constancy.

If Madame des Ursins had suffered sometimes from what she regarded as wearisome ceremonial in Rome, she must have found the etiquette of the Spanish Court of a nature that tried her patience deeply, as, indeed, it would that of anyone unaccustomed to its capricious vagaries and to the extraordinary conceits and senseless ceremonies by which all that bore on the royal family was surrounded. That of the French Court was sufficiently pompous to content anyone, however deeply steeped in the love of order and ostentation, but that of the Spanish Court usurped the place of reason and sense, while its pretentious parade necessarily diminished the dignity of the occasion it pretended to illustrate, or the personage it professed to honour. Madame des Ursins had hated and resisted the abuse of ceremonial at Rome, but at Madrid she could not but accept it, with some irritation it is true, though tempered by considerable amusement at the absurdity in which the situation often resulted. Religion was found to be as good a peg as many others whereon to hang the desired ordinances, and the Princess, who at this time kept up a constant and animated correspondence with Torcy, gives a lively description of an instance. On the 'Jour de la Conception,' soon after their arrival at Madrid, the King and Queen went to High Mass at the large church. The evening before, it was necessary to arrange all the details of the ceremony, 'and while,' said she, 'their majesties were honouring me with the description of the particulars, there suddenly entered the room a malicious little old monkey, about whom I must tell you. This little old monkey is called the Patriarch of the Indies, and is a high dignitary of the church. The King inquired who was to hold the tablecloth while the Queen and himself received, to which the little old monkey replied that the late King had always received alone, and that it was himself who performed that part of the ceremony, but that as the Queen was to be there—a fact of which he evidently highly disapproved—it must fall to himself and to me to perform those duties, and to present the cup. As soon as he had left the room, I repre-

sented to their majesties that it would not be decent
for me to exhibit myself at the altar with a patriarch
before the whole world, for, if the ceremony were an
ecclesiastical one, I could not take part in it, and if it
were otherwise, I had better have someone with me.
The King assented, and sent to tell the patriarch that
he was to hand the cup, and that I and the Duc de
Benavente must hand the cloth. The prelate to this
simply replied that it was impossible, assigning however no reason for his opinion, nor any other message.
When, therefore, the time came, the Duc de Benavente
took up the cloth and approached the Queen, but with
great celerity and dexterity the little prelate whipped
another out of his pocket—one so infinitesimal in its
dimensions that it was hardly able to reach across
from the King to the Queen.' The King was angry,
the Queen surprised, and Madame des Ursins, we may
be sure, considerably irritated. The whole matter was
laid before the council, while the King refused to take
any decisive step without the sanction of Pontocarrero.
We may observe that indignant as was Madame des
Ursins at the patriarch's arrogance, she herself was no
less jealous than he of what she considered her special
right. The whole ceremony cannot have gained much
in solemnity or dignity by the quarrels of these old
people. Not only this, but that very same day—we
suppose that it was one of the first appearances of the
sovereigns after their installation in Spain, and that
thus everything would be used as a precedent—that
very same day another unseemly exhibition of jealous

rivalry took place between two of the nobles of Philippe's Court and desecrated the church under whose roof it took place with its ignominious venom. The brush of the morning had probably roused the pugnacity of the lovers of etiquette, and they seemed to have been inspired to go and do likewise, for just as their majesties were approaching the prie-dieu, on which they were to perform their devotions, the Major-Domo Conte Puego seized hold of it, and at one and the same moment the Duc d'Ossuna precipitated himself eagerly forward to reach it from out of the presumptuous hands of the invader, or, rather from those of the person he regarded as such, and at the very foot of the altar the controversy raged with unholy fury, Puego being resolved not to let go his hold, while d'Ossuna, who was (Madame des Ursins observed) no bigger than a good-sized rat, was within a hair's-breadth of being pitched over, prie-dieu and all, upon the King's person, and the King upon the Queen. The oddest thing of all is, said Madame des Ursins, that both combatants are of the most peaceable dispositions possible, and without the smallest inclination to quarrel on any other subject in the whole world.

CHAPTER V

IN the meantime the Emperor Leopold had no intention of submitting to the decision arrived at by the deceased King Charles of Spain, and he opened the War of Succession in Italy in the spring of 1701. William III., King of England, although his health was rapidly declining and his days drawing to a close, was too eager to crush his old enemy Louis, not to enter heart and soul into any device to overwhelm him. He hastened all preparations to join in the attack, but death was first in the race, and claimed the avenging monarch, frustrating his gallant resolution to place himself, in spite of his enfeebled condition, at the head of his army. England had promised forty thousand men besides her fleet, and she stood honourably to her word. Thus there was a formidable array against Philippe, for the House of Austria had a good many partizans in some of the provinces, while Catalonia showed more than a barren wish to support the Archduke Charles, the Emperor's candidate and son. The Duke of Savoy, the father-in-law of the King of Spain, and allied to the French throne by a like connection, began to show signs of infidelity to both monarchs. He required and expected more emolument from France—more advantages than he seemed likely to extract even from these two magnificent alliances, to obtain one of which he had already forsaken the cause of Austria. He was not treated with the con-

sideration that he conceived he merited. Voltaire
says that the French ministers and generals slighted
him, their attitude implying, as he justly inferred, that
his sons-in-law made but little account of him ; he expected and hoped for some grants of land from Louis,
but the French King did not see it in the same light.
He kept his possessions closely, and had no intention
of bestowing any such substantial mark of his favour
on the Duke, probably remembering, and justly concluding, that he had abandoned the Empire for France
when interest demanded it, and would abandon France
for the Empire when circumstances presented a different face. And, indeed, the Emperor promised him
much larger bribes than ever France had done, both
in lands and moneys. Portugal also at this time for-
sook France, and in 1702 John Churchill, afterwards
Duke of Marlborough, was declared Generalissimo of
the English troops. Prince Eugéne, the son of Louis'
first love, Olympe Mancini, had joined the Emperor
as early as 1685, on the occasion of Louis refusing
him a regiment. He had been one of the insubordinate princes who at that time had fled from Paris to
fight for Germany, declaring that the King refused to
permit them to distinguish themselves at home. It
was on this occasion that Louis had shown much
dignity and magnanimity, for he had been shocked
and hurt at finding that his own child, married to the
young Prince de Conti, was leagued against him with
the rebellious and ungrateful princes of whom he
(Conti) was also one. The King recalled them all, all

but Eugéne, who was forbidden to return. 'I *will* return in spite of him,' said the resentful and mortified Eugéne—and truly he had his revenge. Thus it will be seen that the array against France and Spain was a formidable one indeed.

PART II

CHAPTER VI

THE story of Madame des Ursins is so entirely dependent on the history of Europe that we must be forgiven if we shortly recapitulate the embroiled and somewhat curious condition in which the War of Succession plunged the whole Continent. The enormous conquests of Spain under her former sovereigns, the possession of Sicily, Sardinia, Naples, the Netherlands, Franche Comté and Milan, the conquest of Mexico, and Peru, and the acquisition of Portugal had made her the preponderating power of Europe; but the War of Succession was the tocsin of her downfall. France had watched her aggrandisement with jealous eyes, and Louis, as soon as Mazarin was in his grave, had pursued a similar policy of acquisition. For seventy-two years he reigned, and during by far the greater part of that time he carried on war. From 1661 to 1715, when he died, he owned no will but his own, he guided France with his own hand, steeped her in war, exhausted her finances, and became what every despotic sovereign does become, unless he is

46

possessed of a mind of extraordinary power and almost superhuman wisdom—an arbitrary, irresponsible, deluded ruler. Louis believed that it was the duty of France to represent him, rather than that he should represent France; yet although his views were distorted, it cannot be denied that sometimes his opinions stood him in good stead. According to his lights, he maintained the dignity of the Empire, and he encouraged the arts and sciences.

The Spaniards at the death of Charles II., seeing themselves threatened with war by the Emperor, had yielded up all into the hands of France, and both the Spanish Netherlands and the Duchy of Milan were garrisoned by French troops.

The French fleet came to Cadiz, a squadron was sent to the West Indies, and thus the whole of the Spanish Empire fell into the hands of Louis. At this time the Duke of Burgundy had no children, and it appeared likely that the two countries, France and Spain, would be eventually united under one crown, and the seventeenth century closed with as threatening a prospect for Europe as it is possible to imagine. Nation was rising against nation, but Louis' power, although apparently increasing, was by no means well-assured. Philippe gave notice of his accession to all the European Courts and announced his intention of supporting the claims of the Pretender to the throne of England, and so confusion reigned in the Dutch army, while the French occupied the Spanish Netherlands, and no one knew who was master. Treaties were set

at naught, the Pope favoured the French, the Venetians
the Emperor, and the latter determined to send an
army to Italy under Prince Eugéne.

Madame des Ursins was well pleased when, in 1702,
the Spanish King left Madrid to join his army in
Italy to resist the invasion of the Emperor. She
understood that in order to gain over him the ascendency she deemed necessary, she must first obtain
influence over the Queen. The latter was made
Regent for the term of her husband's absence, and
the Camerera watched her pupil jealously and carefully. Daily she attended the meetings of the
' Junte,' at the head of which she was placed, Pontocarrero acting as president. Under the pretext of
chaperoning her majesty, the Princess watched,
observed, studied and initiated herself into the ways
and customs of that assembly. The young Queen
was only then in her fifteenth year, and became, as
was perfectly natural, wax in the hands of her teacher.
She was of a very intelligent and somewhat pre-
cocious nature, still, a young girl of that age was not
likely to retain much power of volition in the hands
of so experienced, artful and able a conspirator, as
Madame des Ursins. Besides yielding her her will,
the Queen gave her her devoted affection, and as
time went on and the child learnt all the intricacies,
arts, intrigues and cabals of the Court, she continued
to place herself unreservedly under the guidance of
her ruler, and was content to be entirely subject to
her authority. She relied upon her for everything—

for instruction—for amusement—and for her daily
well-being. The King, the direction of whose conduct was, of course, the object of Madame des Ursins'
ambition, was also that of the Queen's love. He was
entirely ruled by his wife, to whom he was passionately attached, and as Madame des Ursins realised
the absolute power that might, through the incapacity
of the one and the inexperience of the other, become
hers, higher and higher grew her ambition. Cardinal
Pontocarrero and the Marquis de Rivas were the
leaders of the 'Junte,' and Madame des Ursins kept
Madame de Maintenon aware of the details of their
deliberations and of the doings of the Spanish Court,
—at least of such as she thought it desirable she
should know—at the same time carefully avoiding
all appearance of personal interference. It was
Madame de Maintenon's fixed resolution to know
all that was being done at Madrid, and she herself
was one of the most important forces with which
the Princess had to reckon. The latter had the
enormous advantage of being herself on the theatre
of war, while the Pyrénées, of the collapsibility of
which Louis had so confidently prated, lay between
the two players of this complicated game of chess.
But the distance was too wide, the time taken up in
communications too great for Madame de Maintenon
to be able to watch the *finesse* of the moves and the
details of the history as it travelled swiftly along the
grooves of time. 'Les absens ont toujours tort,' and
she lost her way in the labyrinth that was created by

D

one yet more artful than herself. Madame des
Ursins possessed the refined power of making her
adversary believe that it was she — Madame de
Maintenon—who really directed the councils of
Spain ; while she—Madame des Ursins—only responded to her teaching. Hence the intimacy between these two remarkable women—both ambitious,
both artful, both unscrupulous—each bent on having
her own way, and one completely duped.

During Philippe's absence at Naples, the English
fleet had glided threateningly along the Spanish coast,
and the young Queen, animated as she was by a great
desire to establish her husband's throne, and to gain
the affection of the Spanish people, did all she could
to inspire them to defend the monarchy. She offered
ner jewels,—this little girl of fourteen,—to help to pay
the army, and a feeling of admiration and affection
was called forth by her spirited conduct. Although
she was, of course, acting under the superintendence
of the Camerera-Major, she was an apt, intelligent,
and responsive pupil, realising better than many of
double her age how much depended on her, while
Madame des Ursins, so subtle in diplomacy, so far-
seeing and resolute in action, found little difficulty in
training to her own method a flower that, transplanted
from its own soil, had taken such kindly root under
her fostering care. So, when the British ships appeared in the Spanish main, and the Queen convoked
the council, and appealed to the loyalty of its members,
all present responded satisfactorily to the invocation.

During the early days of Philippe's reign, it had become obvious that unless every branch of the state were administered with some sort of capacity, entire bankruptcy must ensue. Pontocarrero acknowledged the necessity of reconstruction, and the urgency of the case was laid before Louis. There was a man in Paris named Orry, who had shown much aptitude for finance in Geneva, and who was patronised by Louis' minister, Chamillard. Orry was a man of ability, partaking somewhat of the character of a Chevalier d'Industrie. He had tried his 'prentice hand at many things, and amongst others had undertaken to manage the affairs of the Duchess of Portsmouth, who, finding that he cheated her, had dismissed him. He had had dealings, however, with some financiers, whose commissions he had executed so much to their satisfaction that he was recommended by them to Chamillard. When, therefore, Louis consulted this latter on the money difficulties of Spain, Chamillard proposed that Orry should be sent to Madrid to investigate matters and to suggest remedies for a condition of affairs that could not be dealt with by anyone from a distance. Madame des Ursins recognised the urgency of the case, received Orry cordially, and a strong compact and alliance of friendship was formed between the two. Orry at once assumed the direction of financial and commercial matters; his assistance, friendship and confidence proved of great advantage to her, and assured her of a means whereby she learned all the intricacies

and detail of finance, upon which, of course, the whole
welfare and the very existence of the state depended.
The King and Queen supported her friendship with
Orry as, however they would have supported any
action of Madame des Ursins, and Orry was admitted
to the secret conferences which took place in her
apartments, which always followed the meetings of
the Despacho ; for, since the King's return from Naples,
this assembly had taken the place of the ' Junte,' only
differing from it in name, and in the presence of the
King and the absence of the Queen, and consequently
of the Camerera-Major. Philippe could decide nothing
alone. He carried every question to the two women,
and at those conclaves all resolutions were made. In
other words, Madame des Ursins' and Orry's decisions
were discussed between themselves, and afterwards
carried *nem. con.*

A little later on, and another enjoyed the *entrée* to
this little *comité*, where everything was debated and
decided. This was one d'Aubigny, a tall and handsome fellow, who occupied the post of ' Intendant ' in
the household of Madame des Ursins. It was
rumoured that they were on very intimate terms. A
blustering, bold man, loosely knit in body and mind,
swaggering in manner and appearance, a curious
and rather awkward incident proved the scandal of
their equivocal relations to be by no means without
foundation. One evening the Camerera-Major, desiring to have a few words in private with the Duc de
Medina-Coeli and the Marquis de Louville, led the

way to her own apartment. While still in conversation with them she entered the room, followed by the two gentlemen-in-waiting. At the further end, engaged in writing, sat d'Aubigny at a large table. Madame des Ursins went in first, and probably more or less covered the entrance of the other two, for d'Aubigny, only just glancing up, burst into a string of oaths, asking her, with violent expletives, whether he was never to be left an hour's peace, applying at the same time words so coarse and insolent, and with an impetuosity so brusque and insulting, that the whole position was revealed before the Princess could catch his eye and make him a sign to be silent. The Princess recovered herself first. She coloured, laughed, and, in order to bring before him the fact that they were not alone: 'Gentlemen,' she said very loudly, 'd'Aubigny does not like to be disturbed, you see, and assuming an air of authority, she desired him to leave them and he could finish his business later. Looking up, the terrible error he had made flashed upon d'Aubigny, and, apologising confusedly, he left the room. Such a disclosure as this was not likely to remain a secret, and, of course, no doubt of their mutual relations remained. The extraordinary part of the story is that the conference, after the first few minutes of amazed stupefaction, took place all the same, and very shortly after d'Aubigny had apartments assigned to him in the palace. Those of the Infanta Maria-Theresa, the late wife of Louis XIV., were selected, but deemed insufficient for so important an official, and several rooms were added to them for his convenience.

There was a young noble who had been placed about Philippe's person at an early age, of the name of Louville, in the capacity of ' manin,' or '*gentilhomme de la manche.*' This office, occupation, rank, or quality —it is really very difficult to diagnose its composition, or define its drift—resulted from a time-honoured custom that obtained at the French Court that no *enfant de France* should be permitted to walk about —even from his or her earliest and most staggering stage of tottering and helpless infancy—in the fashion suggested by nature, nurses and common-sense ; that is to say, with his or her hand in the supporting clasp of guardian, tutor, or whatever the protecting person might be. A compromise for cases of immediate necessity was made, by permitting the unhallowed person to grasp the wrist of the sacred child, and it was thus that the name came into use ; probably later as sometimes happens, it became the appellation of some particular attendant, without much reference to existing relations.

Louville had been permitted to accompany Philippe to Spain, and had been nominated chief of his French household. His intimacy with the young King had alarmed the watchful and jealous Camerera-Major, who resolved not to admit even the possibility of a rival. On his return with Philippe, he found that the Queen (ostensibly) had established a rule that no gentlemen-in-waiting were to be boarded and lodged in the palace, and that many other privileges had been abolished. Thus commenced the war upon the Marquis de Louville, who, besides being in possession of the King's favour, was a man of intelligence and intellect, therefore she felt it was desirable to get rid of him. St Simon declares that with this ultimate resolve in her mind, she paid him assiduous court, intriguing at the same time for his dismissal. Louville, too, was on terms of intimacy with Torcy, who had now become her antagonist and enemy, and her unerring instinct warned her that in him she might find a dangerous rival. Before the end of 1703, then, Madame des Ursins' manœuvres were rewarded by the recall of the object of her fears.

CHAPTER VII

AT this time both Pontocarrero and d'Estrées, the latter of whom had been appointed French Ambassador at Madrid, and who was invested with a good deal of power by Louis, began to feel somewhat alarmed. Philippe was entirely subjugated by Madame des Ursins, he appealed to her judgment in all things ; the Queen did the same, the courtiers, in spite of repressed anger and jealousy, bowed down before her ; and so the Princess became the pivot upon which turned all things, both political and social. Her rise had been so rapid, her ascendency had become so com-

plete, her assumption of the reins of government had
been so unequivocal and unhesitating, that she lost
something of that balance of mind which is so necessary to those who soar high. She was intoxicated
with the draught of power that she was swallowing,
and she was resolved to govern absolutely. Simple
influence did not content her, and this Pontocarrero
and d'Estrées discovered too late. They had foolishly
relied on their old intimacy and friendship with her,
on the obligations which she owed them, and on the
influence which d'Estrées wielded at the French Court,
together with the *prestige* which surrounded the name
of Pontocarrero. The latter had decided the tenor of
Charles II.'s will, and had been twice invested with
absolute power in Spain; thus they had both felt an
unwise security in their own influence, and to be sup-
planted by a woman—and that woman a lady-in-
waiting — was almost too much for the intriguing
Frenchman and the proud Castillian to endure.

Madame des Ursins was resolved to defeat the
two cardinals, who were unable to conceal their present hostility. She could not dismiss them herself,
although we rather wonder that she did not strain her
power and attempt to do so, but she was not the less
resolved that they should go. Pontocarrero, arrogant
and furious, chafed under the yoke; was he to be thus
humiliated by a woman and a foreigner? Helpless in
the Despacho as elsewhere, insulted and mortified at
every turn, he at last angrily quitted the Council. She
had altered its hours, changed its ceremonies, inter-

fered with its time-honoured customs ; so intolerable, in short, were her persecutions, so incapable of retaliation and self-defence were her victims, that with hatred and fury in his heart, Pontocarrero finally actually quitted Madrid. Open war was then declared between her and d'Estrées. Madame des Ursins feigned, to the consternation of the King and Queen, to desire to retire to Italy. The Spanish ministry made every effort to support d'Estrées, seeing the government of Spain slipping from their grasp ; but Madame de Maintenon at this crisis, when Louis was appealed to by both sides, warmly took her part, warning the French King of the disasters she was sure would befall if Madame des Ursins left Madrid. Cardinal d'Estrées, continually quarrelling with her, could bear it no more ; his position was insupportable, and he asked for his recall. But the Spanish ministry succeeded in gaining one point, viz., that his nephew, the Abbé, who had been associated with his uncle in his embassy, should remain as ambassador, and although the Princess could not endure the peremptoriness of the condition, she and Madame de Maintenon thought it prudent to submit ; besides, they believed that the Abbé would not dare to resist Madame des Ursins as determinedly as his uncle. Philippe had let Louville go without much resistance, and thus Madame des Ursins and Orry remained masters of the situation, obtaining a degree of personal power hardly ever surpassed, even in Spain. There was no one to dispute their authority ; their will was supreme. Any French persons who had lingered about

the Spanish Court at this time, returned to their native
country, except one or two who had never questioned
her authority.　The Despacho had practically ceased
to exist, for, in order to destroy even the semblance of
any domination but her own, the Princess had decreed
that the hour of meeting should be ten p.m., in order
further to confuse and fatigue the old men who princi-
pally composed it, and she administered the various
departments of War, Home and Foreign Affairs precisely as she saw fit.

Thus, at this time, she reigned indeed.　She had
conquered the cardinals, dismissed Louville, and
routed all who were either obstacles to her power or
likely to become so, or who enjoyed the smallest
portion of the King's favour, independently of her
own.　She was, in short, master of King, Queen,
State, Court and of all that appertained to Spain.

The cardinal gone, she resolved to try and make
use of his nephew the Abbé, who had acted with his
uncle as a species of assistant or secretary, but it is said
to be the fact that although he was so left, and acted
in the capacity of ambassador, her power and influence
were so great that she actually exacted his promise
that he would never send letter or despatch to Paris
without her concurrence and supervision.　The Abbé
naturally fretted under these humiliating conditions,
and, we suppose, showed his restlessness under the
curb, and she, beginning to suspect his fidelity, and
that he was not true to his promise, resolved to put
the case to the proof.　A struggle became imminent.

There are different accounts as to the manner in which she became possessed of the unlucky despatch, the story of which was so fraught with dire consequences to herself. Louville says that Orry took it to her, having promised d'Estrées to send it off under his own cover. Berwick asserts that the Princess induced Philippe to have it violently seized and wrested from the courier. But in whatever manner she obtained possession of it, certain it is that a terrible scandal resulted, from the consequences of which she only emerged after many penalties and much anguish. The Abbé, tingling with fury at all the indignities heaped upon him by this arrogant woman, the scourge of the whole Court and ministry, had written a long account of the wrongs suffered by them all, to Louis. Unless she were crushed, he declared she would annihilate everyone. The cardinal, his uncle, had just arrived at the French Court, from Madrid. 'Now,' thought the Abbé, 'is the moment to effect our purpose.' Madame des Ursins recognised the deduction as well as the Abbé. She resolved to steal the despatch, and to apprise herself, by its perusal, of what she was to expect. It was brought to her. When she opened it, she read a history of her life at Court, as it appeared to others; her actions were summarised, her words criticised, her arrogance and insolence displayed, together with an account of the insults she had heaped on her betters. We may be sure that nothing was omitted that would tend to blacken her in the eyes of Louis and of Madame de Maintenon. Her manœuvres were

chronicled, she was, he said, all-powerful with
the King, and he thereupon sketched the young
monarch's Court with a free hand. Despotic, tyrannical, and absolute, there was but one exception that
marked her dealings with others, and that, said the
candid and communicative ambassador, was in the
case of Boutrot d'Aubigny, the Princess's own intendant, and here the position was reversed. The
Princess, he declared, was subject to, and ruled by
him ; and he repeated with detail and sundry com-
ments all the scandal that was current in Madrid
regarding her,—scandal that had attached itself to
her name by her own indifference to appearances,
and even decencies,—adding at the same time, possibly
with a charitable intention of mitigating the scurrility
of the particulars, that it was 'popularly believed they
were married.' The Princess read all the accusations
directed against her political actions, her social habits,
and her offensive and arrogant demeanour, with indifference not unmixed with interest and, possibly,
with some amusement. She was not in the least
mortified even at the scandal that coupled her name
with that of d'Aubigny, but the imputation of marriage
seems to have angered her so inconceivably, and to
have caused her such passionate indignation and
offence, that, seizing a pen, she wrote furiously on the
margin of the paper, '*Pour mariés non !*' The
missive was forwarded to its addressee the King of
France, thus annotated with more decision than
discretion and more anger than decency.

Surely never before was disclaimer in three short, sharp words so convincingly, so succinctly, so concisely conveyed! The special allegation that had fired her indignation and set her anger ablaze, she disposed of, closed it as it were, with a final and decisive snap, while all the other imputations were nearly as eloquently avowed and as convincingly acknowledged by her contemptuous silence. 'All the rest if you will,' implied the angry Princess—'*mais pour mariés non !*'

Both Louis and Madame de Maintenon were to the last degree scandalised. Thus to break open and annotate a despatch to the King was in itself an offence of marked and extraordinary disrespect, and besides, Louis, like many another convert, was in no degree mollified or softened towards faults and vices of which he himself had been once guilty. His previous errors and present decorum taught him in no way to condone the faults of others. It was many years since he had resigned himself and his conscience into the unspotted hands of Madame de Maintenon, and the unblushing disclaimer amazed them both. Madame des Ursins' anger had evidently been so great as to overcome her fear of his wrath, and the annotated margin, whose vigorous negation on one point proclaimed the truth of other portions of the accusation, was probably very little in Louis' mind, in comparison to the indignity offered to himself, enacted by opening his sacred despatch. And certainly it was an offence as reprehensible as it was insolent, and one cannot help

wondering that the Camerera's sagacity, which as a
rule was great, permitted her to write her own condemnation on the margin of an official document. Louis
was beginning to have a little further insight into
matters at Madrid, and Madame des Ursins' marginal
utterances found him in no mood to condone so grave
an impropriety. He wrote to her in terms of the
highest displeasure of her unpardonable indiscretion
in opening a despatch addressed to himself, but to her
the bitterest part of all was that d'Estrées was made
acquainted with the reprimand. Naturally he crowed
with all his might and main at this triumph over his
insolent enemy, and took all the means in his power
to spread abroad a result so soothing to his pride.

For Madame des Ursins now, matters began to look
a little threatening ; Louis' faith in her had received
some rather rude shocks. The attitude of the Court
of Madrid he thought was not wholly satisfactory.
Early in 1704 (at which date we have now arrived) he
had wished his grandson to march on Portugal, which
country had thrown off its allegiance to Spain the
year before. But England had interfered and ham-
pered French interests while Madame des Ursins'
tactics had not pleased him. She had asked for
Berwick to command the troops rather than a Frenchman—he was a Jacobite, and the illegitimate son of
our James II., poor, and desirous of taking a place
amongst the French aristocracy as Duc de Fitz-
James, and Louis had yielded to her desire. He
had nominated Puységur (who preceded Berwick into

Spain) as second in command. Orry had assured the latter that magazines and all the necessary preparations for war were complete, but Puységur, on going through the country, found nothing ready, and indignantly wrote the truth to the French King, for not one town or fortification was in a fit state for siege. This disclosure being made to Louis just about the same time as the incident of the annotated despatch, filled that monarch with indignation and alarm, while the two d'Estrées pressed home all the implied censure against Madame des Ursins. Nevertheless, the Abbé's position at Court was fast becoming not only intolerable but incompatible with his dignity as ambassador, for the Queen was acting in his enemy's interests and under her instructions. But d'Estrées had been a little in advance of his legitimate triumph, a little too eager to proclaim the amount of his success; he sang too loudly before he was out of the wood, and was none the better of his boasted advantage. Indeed, his fall came before hers. She possessed, as we have seen, Madame de Maintenon's ear, which was the passport to Louis' confidence, and thus, for the present at least, she still held her own.

The dreaded notice to quit had not arrived, and Estrées, smarting under the disappointment, angry and puzzled at so meagre a result, after so hopeful and promising a beginning, believing that a *coup d'état* would yield what he desired, rashly sent in his resignation, believing this action would hasten the punishment he felt sure was about to fall on the arrogant

Princess. To his dismay, it was accepted. This
event of course caused *her* the liveliest joy; Louis,
however, was not so easily appeased. Madame des
Ursins and Orry had forfeited his confidence, and he
had taken his resolution, but also his time to carry it
out. D'Estrées hastily retired from Madrid, unable
to face the insolent triumph of the Princess, to say
nothing of the Queen's unconcealed satisfaction.
Louis intended that both should quit Spain, but he
knew enough about the way in which things were
conducted in Madrid to feel very doubtful whether
his orders would be as promptly executed, as he desired. The distance was great; time must elapse
before he could calculate on replies to his communications and he knew the Princess to be a woman of courage and resource, the Queen was her devoted follower,
Philippe that of both, and Louis wisely decided not to
act till he could be sure of his orders being instantly
carried into effect. Therefore, having despatched the
reprimand which had so rejoiced d'Estrées' vengeful
heart, he had paused. Although he accepted the
Abbé's resignation, it did not follow that the Princess
would get off scot free. The annotated despatch, and
the information concerning the unprepared state of
Spain for war, had arrived almost simultaneously, and
even Madame de Maintenon found some difficulty in
defending her *protégée;* while the latter, not knowing of the rod which was in pickle for her, began to
triumph in her turn. There were, however, drawbacks
to her supposed success which was by no means as

complete as she had begun to believe. The cardinal
was furious at the turn matters seemed taking, and demanded compensation for the insults which had been
heaped on himself and his nephew. Some manœuvring procured for the latter the order of the St Esprit,
one very rarely granted to an abbé, and therefore
apparently a twofold mark of Louis' favour ; he also
promised him the first vacant ecclesiastical *cordon
bleu*, and displayed his eagerness to bestow it on him
by despatching it the moment he heard of the death
of Cardinal Fürstenburg. Not only this, but the
Abbaye of St Germain des Près was accorded to him.
These rich gifts contented the Abbé mightily, and he
did not hesitate to avow publicly that a great part of
this joy proceeded from the knowledge of Madame
des Ursins' anger and disappointment.

The truth was that Louis was too wary to act
hastily in a crisis on the result of which so much
depended, and now his diplomacy came into play.

A war with Portugal, in spite of Orry's neglect
as to the necessaries for the campaign, was begun,
and Philippe was desirous of making it in person,
while Madame des Ursins was unwilling to lose sight
of and therefore, possibly, control over him. In every
wish expressed or step taken, the Queen supported
her, but Louis came to his grandson's aid, and not
only confirmed him in his desire, but commanded him
to carry it out, while Madame des Ursins and the
Queen made arrangements to accompany him. Louis
was determined, however, that the struggle now begun

E

should end in the defeat of the two women, and his
instructions were so peremptory that they were compelled to yield, and the Queen and the Camerera
remained in Madrid, while Philippe headed his troops
and went away in the month of March. Thus far
Louis had carried out his intentions. But there still
remained to exile the Princess. No sooner was the
Spanish King gone, than Louis wrote commanding
her to quit Madrid immediately, and to retire to
Rome. In similar terms he wrote to the Queen about
the Princess, and also to Philippe, who was already
beginning the campaign, and thus unable to be approached by his wife. The Queen was in despair. She
felt that her only friend, her almost mother, was being
torn from her. She had no friend but her; the King
was away, and she wept and sobbed, and wrung her
hands at the dreary prospect. She implored the
French King at least to grant the Princess a hearing
for the purpose of justification, and perhaps this
appeal ultimately helped to induce Louis to permit
the degraded Camerera to visit him.

These reverses, however, only caused Madame des
Ursins to brace herself up, and arm herself for battle,
—to buckle on her armour, and face the enemy with
undaunted mien. An old and adroit hand, as we have
seen, in the science of diplomacy, she had grasped and
understood all Louis' tactics, and how that it was the
annotated despatch that had brought things to this
crisis. She took thought for the morrow and accepted
the situation for to-day. She realised that disobedi-

ence would mean permanent destruction, so she laid
her counter plans. She faced all the difficulties and
held her ground in Madrid till she could do so no
longer. At last the decisive blow came in the shape
of a peremptory order for her to retire immediately to
Italy, while Orry was to betake himself to Paris.
Characteristically daring and defiant, she refused, in
spite of the advice of the Marquis de Chateauneuf
(Louis' envoy in the matter) to go to Italy, and went
by slow stages to Vittoria, whence she wrote to the
Maréchale de Noailles a letter, dated May 22d, 1704,
which lifts a small corner of the veil and discloses
some of the anger and passion that were almost con-
suming her. 'Lies have overwhelmed the truth,' she
says, 'no one will ever serve the King with more truth
and fidelity than I have done, but I am treated as a
criminal who has betrayed the state, and my accusers
triumph! Artificial and wretched men, like the
d'Estrées, can easily contrive a cabal against a woman
who has no support but that of a grand honesty of
purpose, but that those who had assured her of their
friendship should plot against her—those,' she says
sarcastically, 'she really admires!' She appeals to
her friend—is she of this number she asks, and with
mortification and mistrust bubbling out of every
reproachful word, she inquires passionately how such
treatment of her own—Madame de Noailles'—relation
does not horrify and insult her? 'Tout ce que je puis
vous dire pour me défendre' she says, 'c'est qu'on
vous a trompé.' Does she know the d'Estrées as she

(Madame des Ursins) knows them, she continues, and
in words whose indignant agitation is only the more
visible by reason of their obvious restraint, she re-
proaches her correspondent with the difference of the
nature of the friendship which she bears to her—'Per-
mettez-moi les reproches, madame,' she says in dignified expostulation — 'J'ai encore assez de politesse
pour etre fachée de vous les faire' and as to Madame
de Maintenon, she adds, perhaps somewhat injudi-
ciously (but who can speak with judgment when overwhelmed by the sense of defeat and disgrace?) 'She
knows enough of her to see that she would act neither
for, nor against her, but God,' she concludes with singular confidence and assurance, 'se servira de moi malgré
moi mêne pour faire apparaître mon innocence et
l'imposture de ceux qui me calomnient.' This letter
does not seem to have resulted in the estrangement
that, from so hot an appeal and so intense a feeling of
anger, might have been expected, for another, written
from Toulouse in the same year, softened in tone, less
fierce in spirit and more subdued in tendency, forms
the next of the series.

Although Madame de Maintenon would not compromise herself so far as to write to her former friend,
she worked hard for her reinstatement.

CHAPTER VIII

BEFORE quitting Madrid, Madame des Ursins acted
with all the prudence and foresight of one who was
only temporarily baffled ; she made all arrangements
for the management of affairs during the term of her
absence ; she inducted the Duchesse de Montillano
as provisionary Camerera-Major, a lady of as mild
and tractable disposition as she herself was the reverse ;
she intended to turn her out on her own certain
return ; she selected one of her own creatures as her
paid spy and to keep her informed of all that was
doing ; she instructed the Queen as to her conduct
in certain contingencies in as great detail as the limited
time for such conferences permitted, and she told her
what measures to take to ensure her own speedy return.　In short, she arranged all the machinery of the
political engines, paid many visits of farewell, preserving profound silence as to the cause of her resignation as she called it, and faced the situation with masculine courage and feminine endurance.　Dignified and
courteous to all, she possessed the rare power of being
able, when she pleased, to steer between haughtiness
and humility.　The Queen was overwhelmed with
grief at the prospect of losing her friend, but she
eagerly and dutifully listened to the instructions that
the Princess gave her in the case of all the contingencies that she could think of.　In short, the
Princess left her house — Spain — in order, and her

servants,—the Queen and the King,—received her commands how to conduct it. No emotion was apparent
to any extraneous person, she remained until every
order had been given, every precaution taken, every
contingency prepared for, and then she took formal
leave of the whole entourage. The queen accompanied
her two miles out of town, then bade her farewell
and went back to Madrid.

The Camerera stopped at a small village called
Alcala, five leagues from the capital, and there stayed
for five weeks—she could not bring herself to quit
the scenes of her triumph, her glories, and of her
despotic sway, and it is said that more than once
during that period she returned to Madrid.

But the time came when she was compelled to go,
and by short and unwilling journeys she at length
arrived at Bayonne. Her fixed intention was to
journey to Bayonne, and from thence to justify her
conduct to the King and to Madame de Maintenon.
Of another thing she was also determined, and that was
that the place of her exile should be France and not
Italy, and of yet another was she equally resolved,
that should she fail of obtaining an audience of the
King now, the time should come when she would do
so in spite of all the cardinals and ambassadors in
Europe.

Although Madame de Maintenon had not opposed
Louis' action with respect to Madame des Ursins, she
very shortly after the dismissal of the latter began to
regret the absence from the Spanish Court of one who

had, as she believed, kept her *au courant* of all the
doings at Madrid. She began therefore to intrigue for
her return thither. Louis had asserted himself, she
argued ; he had covered the two d'Estrées with orders,
appointments, and favours of all sorts. Did not this
suffice? Might the diplomatic lady not return to the
field of her labours ?—labours which she had so profit-
ably conducted. Had not the punishment already exceeded the crime ? Did not her talents and merits out-
weigh her indecorums, her transgressions, her errors?
The Queen, Madame de Maintenon asserted, was too
young for the important position in which she was now
placed, and being quite as ready to strengthen her
arguments with exaggerated praise to gain her ends, as
many another, she cast about for an extenuation of
her friend's conduct. In fact she was resolved that the
Princess should return to her old post ; the King sooner
or later was sure to confirm her will as his own, and
having gone thus far in developing her intentions, she
fixed upon Toulouse as the head-quarters of Madame
des Ursins' exile. No place could have suited the
plans of either better. It was in France—it was close
to the Spanish frontier, and Madame des Ursins could,
if she pleased (but this she would not please), cross
the Alps at any time and find herself in Italy, while
Versailles, if far, was also practicable, as the roads were
good. Toulouse, in short, was the high road to the
fulfilment of her own desires, and at the same time a
centre easily reached by Madame de Maintenon's spies,
a kind of *salle d'attente* where the Princess could stay

and watch and intrigue, as well as a starting point whence she could bend her steps according to circumstances.

So Madame des Ursins travelled slowly from Bayonne to Toulouse. Always manœuvring, always struggling to go no further away from Spain, she hoped if she gained this point, that all the rest would follow, and she was not mistaken. Louis, through Madame de Maintenon's arts, was becoming less embittered against the Princess, and in October 1704, it was rumoured that although she was not to return to Madrid, and although it was the summit of the Queen's ambition that she should do so, this concession had been made—that she was to go to Paris in November. Rumour for once proved correct. Louis sent her a summons or a permit, and in November she bent her steps towards the French capital.

During several months' residence at Toulouse, Madame des Ursins had established regular communications between herself and the Court of Madrid. The Duc de Grammont, who had taken d'Estrées' place there as ambassador, and whose feelings were inimical to the Princess, was hated by the King and Queen, who knew that he was straining every nerve to prevent her return. They thwarted him in every possible way, negatived his counsels and resisted his opinions, while the Queen, still more active in her dislike than her husband, lost no opportunity of annoying him in every conceivable manner. Louis, to whom, of course, De Grammont repeated all his grievances, was furious, but the Queen's deliberate desire was that it should appear to the King that the Princess alone could conduct the affairs of Spain, and thus her return might be hastened. Angry as was the French monarch at the opposition thus deliberately offered to his will, Madame des Ursins held the reins with quite as firm a hand, if with greater difficulty than before. She dictated, and the King and Queen obeyed. In the spring of 1705, Maulevrier, the nephew of Colbert, was entrusted with important letters from the Duchess of Burgundy to her sister the Queen of Spain, and Madame des Ursins believed that these were the *avant-couriers* of her own pardon and reinstatement. She had had reliable information on this head, not only from Madrid, but from France, and in Spain they made a confidant of Maulevrier who aided them with his counsel, and advised the Queen how to proceed for the fulfilment of her desires. While Louis chafed under the continued affronts offered to his representative, Madame de Maintenon was employing her art to gain the latter over to her views. She contrived to half persuade him that the Princess had no design of re-entering Spain, nor, indeed, that she had any mind to do so. She declared to Louis that the Queen's power over her husband was unbounded and undesirable, that it was unrestrained by any other than personal reasons, and that she (the Queen) alone was the cause of the opposition suffered by Grammont. She assured him that it would be expedient that the Princess should return to Spain in his interests, that Madame des Ursins ought to come to Versailles to learn her master's will and pleasure, receive his instructions, and that he should hear her defence and explanation of her previous conduct, when he could, of course, said she, mould her to his irresistible will. And the French King, won by his vanity, was beguiled into believing that it was by his own unassisted wish and original suggestion, not only that he should partially forgive the Princess, but that she should be permitted to break her exile by a journey to Versailles.

D'Harcourt and Madame de Maintenon, under the able generalship of the latter, returned repeatedly to the charge, and the King, to whom no one ever spoke the truth, probably did not realise that if the Princess came to Versailles, her return to Madrid was assured. Still he had been alarmed at the insubordination that had shown itself there, and possibly being more or less convinced by a mind that had always mastered his own, he, through D'Harcourt and Madame de Maintenon, extended his modified pardon to the offending Princess. A courier was instantly despatched to Toulouse with the joyful intelligence that she might not only come to Paris but to the Court, an announcement the triumphant joy of which we can hardly describe. It was, however, on such occasions that the Princess demonstrated what, for want of a better term, we will call the greatness of her character. Always mistress of her feelings, and far exceeding her expectations as was the delightful permission to visit the French Court, she received the news with exactly the same outward calm as distinguished her conduct at Madrid when she learned the sentence of exile. She showed no sign of emotion. She pretended not to be elated, and charged all her followers to imitate her demeanour. She communicated with Madrid, but she displayed no outward haste to depart.

No sooner had the courier left Paris for Toulouse than a rumour spread itself abroad of the mission with which he was charged. All those who had blamed her before seemed desirous of welcoming her back, says St Simon, and on Sunday, January 4, 1705, the victorious and redoubtable lady arrived in the French capital. The Duc and Duchesse d'Albe, the Spanish Ambassador, drove a long way out of the town to meet her and bring her back to the hospitality of their own hotel, and even made her the object of a magnificent *fête*. Paris flocked to see her. All welcomed her with a warmth which left no doubt as to the spirit in which her advent had been announced at Court. Indeed, she must have been as much astonished as delighted at so grand and effusive a welcome, one that her worldly knowledge of course told her could but be the forerunner of triumphant success. All the demonstrations, however, she accepted calmly and as if they were but her due. She presented no appearance of agitation or surprise. Crowds called upon her, Paris was excited, enthusiastic, agitated, curious and diverted. The King sent Torcy, her original friend, to meet her. Torcy was amazed at her triumph, at her calmness and at the confidence of her demeanour. He was himself embarrassed and confused; not so, however, our Princess—she was equal to that and to every other occasion. Now she was haughty and cold, for latterly Torcy had been her enemy. The *genre* of her reception gave her the cue for her behaviour, and her intended humility had given way to confidence, so that by this time she had assumed the bearing of the injured party. She now intended to plead for justice, not pardon, to display resentment instead of repentance—resentment against those who, abusing the confidence of Louis, had drawn down upon her a treatment so scandalous and insulting, and had held up two monarchies to the vulgar spite and odium of a curious world. Louis quitted Paris and went to Versailles on the 10th, and the same day saw Madame des Ursins established in a lodging in that town. Up to that time she had seen neither the King nor Madame de Maintenon; but the next day she dined alone, and proceeded thereafter, by command, to the palace. She was closeted with the King, *tête-à-tête*, for two and a half hours, but the next day he declared that they had not spoken on half of the subjects he had desired. After the first audience of the monarch, she visited the Duchess of Burgundy and Madame de Maintenon, and it was evident she made a favourable impression in both cases.

At the end of a month, Philippe sent a colonel

of Spanish troops, named Pozzobuono, to take his
thanks to his grandfather for receiving the Princess,
and ordered his ambassador, d'Albe, to go thither
with all his *cortége*, to pay a visit of ceremony.

Madame des Ursins announced her intention of remaining until April. She was nearly at the apex of
her ambition, but the word which was to remove the
ban and shoot her back to her old position was as yet
unspoken by the King ; and although no one doubted
that it would be pronounced, the fiat must go forth
before her purposes could be accomplished. She was
visited by monseigneur, by madame, and by all the
royal family, seeing as little of any one else as possible.

CHAPTER IX

THE position of Madame des Ursins, in the meantime,
always improved, as is seen by the fact that, when the
Court went to Marly, she not only accompanied them,
but was this time lodged in the palace, and she had
so insinuated herself in Louis' good graces, that his
majesty paid her the most marked attention. All
his displeasure had vanished, and the dignified
manner in which she received his gracious courtesies,
with just the proper proportions of respect and grace,
were a sight to see. 'An old-fashioned courtesy,'
says St Simon (thus showing our generation how each

member of another recalls that of his own youth, and
deems it as immeasurably superior to the present, as
we do ourselves), 'that savoured of the Court of the
Queen-mother.'

Louis had, probably in consequence of the application of artistic adulation, succumbed. Madame des
Ursins had contrived that all her former misdemean-
ours, grave and unquestioned as they were, should be
condoned. The consideration that he showed her, the
gallantry—in a sense distinct from the grand and
highbred courtesy that he manifested to all and
everyone—were not only the tokens of his forgive-
ness, but the indications of the admirably com-
pounded and skilfully administered flattery, of which
the chief ingredient was the implication that he himself was directing all, and watching the effect of what
he deemed his own adroit observation and unerring
judgment. He was inextricably entangled in Madame
des Ursins' network and manœuvres, and was as
much the victim of her machinations as ever was
fly in a spider's web. Indeed, it is, we believe, true
that, although Madame de Maintenon had never
hitherto suffered from the pangs of jealousy, she not
only experienced some uneasiness at this time, but
she had some cause to do so. Although Madame
des Ursins' return to Madrid had become a matter
of course, it was postponed from day to day. Never
did she appear in public without Louis bestowing upon her by far the greater part of his conversation. He laid himself out to entertain her, he called

her attention to whatever pleased himself, he asked her opinion in matters of taste, he sought her approbation with an air of magnificent gallantry and even flattery, which increased with time, rather than diminished. She was established on a footing of intimacy. She made a third in Madame de Maintenon's apartment, sometimes the King and herself were even *tête-à-tête*. The Court looked on, wondered, admired, envied, flattered her; the royal family surrounded her, courted, and visited her. Was ever triumph so unmitigated, success so absolute, whilst the greatest ladies sought for a word? Her influence was enormous, and all vied, one with the other, for her favour. She attended all the Court festivities, and was a prominent and notable figure. At Marly, where there were constant *fêtes* given by the King, the ballroom was a long and vast salon; at the one end stood the King's *fauteuil*, together with those of King James II. and his Queen, that of the latter being placed between those of the two sovereigns. The Fils de France and the Duc d'Orleans were the only other men admitted to those precincts, while opposite were erected the seats for the guests. But Madame des Ursins was always at Louis' table at supper, and he never desisted in his attentions. Not contented with these evidences of the King's favour, Madame des Ursins, who was full of skilful audacity and tactful ability proclaimed to a prying Court and inquisitive world the success of her efforts to re-establish herself in the King's good graces. The manner in which she achieved this was demonstrative and conclusive, original and significant. It announced intimacy, it sounded a note of triumph, and it gave forth such indication of oneness with the King as perhaps could have been conveyed in no other manner. On the evening of one of the magnificent Court balls, when all the world was paying its *devoirs* to the sovereign, the Princess appeared amongst the courtiers with a little spaniel dog under her arm, while Louis paid her the most marked attentions, and himself frequently caressed the little creature, the unconscious advertisement of her victorious campaign.

The Duc de Grammont meantime occupied a very unpleasant position at Madrid. He saw that before long Madame des Ursins would be reinstated in her old position, and knew well whither her restoration pointed. Since his mission there, her hand had in some ways been conspicuous by its absence, for although the Queen endeavoured to carry out the Princess's programme in all respects, her age, of course, prevented her being capable of guiding and governing with perspicacity. Philippe himself, undecided, in character and habits, though perhaps with more intelligence lurking in him than at first appeared (but quite as much timidity and distrust), could not be entirely satisfactorily ruled by a girl of seventeen. Grammont eagerly desired for Spain a despotic government, and as he knew that despotic measures could not be directed by Philippe, he himself desired to play the principal part and guide the whole. His feelings, then, may be better imagined than described when the fact was burst upon him by the authoritative announcement that Louis had pardoned the Princess, and that to him, Grammont, belonged the duty of announcing the news officially to the Spanish Court. He made an effort to induce Louis to reconsider his decision, but failed. 'We can but bow to your orders,' he says in a letter to the French King, 'but if the Queen is delighted, it is not so with the King.'

He could not conceal his surprise, his mortification and his grief. And he concludes by assuring him that he, Philippe, was secretly rejoicing in the absence of Madame des Ursins and did not desire her return, finishing his confidences by beseeching Louis to keep the secret that he imparted to him. And indeed we believe it was true that the Spanish King had tasted the sweets of comparative independence during the absence of his tyrant, and although, of course, on her return he succumbed to her masterful influence, Philippe would have preferred to reign alone, or through an uninfluenced wife. 'The Queen,' proceeds de Grammont, 'cares neither for music nor conversation, neither for *la chasse* nor *la promenade*, she only desires to rule the King and the country, while Philippe himself has a just and upright spirit, though he is idle, feeble and irresolute, and fears Madame des Ursins to excess; and so long as she is there, he will never be more than a child of six.' He entreats Louis to consider his communication as confidential, except to Madame de Maintenon. The truth was

that Philippe was experiencing the inevitable lot of
every weak man in high places—and, indeed, in others
as well—he was the subject of constant quarrelling,
wrestling, intrigue and manœuvring. He was a tool
in the hands of whoever choose to make it his business
that he should be so. Louis wrote to the Duke:
'Don't you know my grandson ?' he asks contemptu-
ously; 'the very moment he would have you believe
that he is finally determined to overcome all domination, he is at that instant engaged in a correspondence
with the Dauphin to exert his influence that the
Princess may return to Spain, as she is indispensable
for the good administration of affairs'—the fact
was that Philippe was so weak he knew not what
he wished ; he was unfit to sustain any argument,
unable to reason or to insist upon a decided line of
action, and he invariably endorsed the views of the
last speaker.

CHAPTER X

MADAME DES URSINS' intimate friendship with Louis
continued, and doubtless she received from him many
instructions and orders, which, of course, she accepted
respectfully and dutifully, with the full intention of
obeying or not, according to the march of events.
Not only was it clear that she was to be reinstated in
her old post, but she chose her own colleagues. She

obtained Louis' permission for Orry's return, and
selected Amelot as the future French ambassador,
telling the King that the latter would watch over
Orry and see that he did not fall into his old faults.
Philippe's confessor, Daubenton, was replaced by
the père Robinet, who was a devoted follower of
Madame des Ursins, and was also a much more
accommodating ecclesiastic than his predecessor;
while the Chevalier Bourke, an Irish gentleman of
considerable acuteness, was chosen as a species of spy,
to keep Chamillard *au courant* of the Jacobite interests
which were allied with those of France. Orry must
have been jubilant, in no less a degree than his
patroness, for he had been called to account for his
misdoings, and that so sharply, that he only barely
escaped death by the goodwill of Madame de Maintenon. Chamillard himself detested Madame des
Ursins, but he kept his feelings to himself and was
quite willing to accommodate his prejudices to the
opposite ones of Louis and Madame de Maintenon.
'Let us hope,' he wrote to Tessé, 'that Madame
des Ursins, Amelot and Orry will work in concert,
which is so necessary for the interests of the Spanish
monarchy.'

Amelot was ultimately received by the 'Junte' and
by the Queen most graciously, but the greater part
of the Spanish Court resented this new influx of
Frenchmen. But the Princess's triumph in her
power over the young King and Queen now, counted
as nothing in comparison with the enormous gratifi-

cation she experienced when, in her frequent communings with the Grand Monarque, she saw him daily laying down his arms before her, every condition conceded, every desire gratified. Before her return, Orry was, at her request, collecting the Spanish troops and organising the continuation of the War of Succession, to which end Louis sent 200,000 crowns for the benefit of the army.

But still she lingered on, seemingly unable to tear herself from the delights of the French Court. Madame de Maintenon was somewhat feeble in health ; the constant wear and tear of her life was great ; she was never absent from the King for a day, and the whole responsibility of the daily routine of his Court and ministry lay with her, and had done so for many years. There are letters from her hand which point to the mortal *ennui* to which she was a victim. She was getting well up in years, being at this time seventy, and although Madame des Ursins herself was not very many years younger (sixty-three), she probably, in view of the pleasure which the King took in her society, felt some hopes that a vacancy might occur in a position that she would far rather occupy than the deputy, though more despotic, prerogative which she enjoyed in Spain. Chamillard was able to judge what was the state of matters pretty accurately, and when he saw the rapidity with which she was advancing in the King's favour, he placed himself at her feet and wisely adjusted himself to the circumstances.

Madame des Ursins at last became aware that some

step must be taken, else she might lose both positions. She therefore began one day, during one of her intimate conversations with Louis, to explain. She alluded to the manner in which she had been expelled Spain with all the ignominy, she said, of a criminal. She hesitated to reappear where she could not do so with honour. Reputation and dignity were indispensable, were she to continue to serve the two kings. Something must be done to proclaim Louis' confidence, and although she was overwhelmed by the kindnesses of his majesty here, those things were not understood in Spain, and in order that they should be so, some public act of the nature of a proclamation, or that might receive the dignity and importance of a formal mission, should celebrate her return to Madrid. These words spoke Madame des Ursins to the King and to Madame de Maintenon at Marly with much apparent ease and some eloquence, and, having finished her speech, she took leave of them, asking permission to see them once more before returning to Versailles. She was resolved to get her desire accomplished before quitting France; and once more she was received at Marly, and on this occasion obtained all that she asked for. Twenty thousand livres were granted her as a pension, in addition to what she had before, and forty thousand for the expenses of the journey, besides the elevation of her brother to the dignity of cardinal.

Having gained all she asked, she quitted France in July 1705, and was a month on the way back.

Thus departed from the French Court one whose

humilation the King of France had planned and compassed in such a way that it was hardly possible for
anyone to be disgraced and dishonoured more deeply ;
and now from—shall we say mere caprice, he had
reversed his tactics, restored her by a stroke of the pen
to her former grandeur, multiplying it an hundred-
fold, had bestowed upon her the old confidence,
and invested her with fresh honours and new favours.
Truly, if Louis was in the habit of reviewing his
actions, he must have felt ashamed of his own only
one year ago, or else of those which he·had just
perpetrated.

But she had conquered him, bent him, subdued
him to her iron will—what wonder, then, that one
so successful and unscrupulous should dare to dream
of greater ambitions? She was more resolute than
ever, and determined to extirpate every vestige of
influence but her own at Madrid, for small naturally,
the result of all these events was an accession of
arrogance and resolution, and a feeling of unmitigated
triumph.

She departed, overwhelmed with confidential communications and other marks of the Royal favour.
Her position in France was incomparably higher than
before, her credit had been rising every day since her
first audience with the great King, and in addition to all
this, every place in the Spanish Court was in her gift.
Absolute power was hers, when exulting and flushed
with victory in August 1705 she entered Spain.

PART III

CHAPTER XI

THE Princess's return to Madrid partook of the nature of a state pageant. She passed through Bordeaux, whose archives still possess the curious details of the extraordinary public and enthusiastic welcome which was accorded her. Princes and magnates, deputies and officials, all dressed in their state uniforms, flew to meet and do her homage, as if she were a royal sovereign returning to take her place on the throne. The town complimented her officially, through gorgeously dressed deputies. Popular *fêtes* were given in her honour, and when she condescended to express a wish to see the peasants dance a *basque*, enthusiasm rose to its height. At St Jean de Luz, the King's carriage, which had arrived several days before to greet the returning exile, awaited her. Regiments quartered there, headed by their colonels, crowded to do her honour. Princes and peasants saluted her, a number of the nobility sent their

carriages to meet her and follow in her wake. Bull-
fights, fireworks, *feux-de-joie*, and acclamations surrounded and pursued the gratified Princess; flowers
were strewn before her carriage, crowds preceded
her, crowds followed her, clergy, magistrates—none
and nothing was wanting to swell her train and complete her triumph. The nearer she approached
Madrid, so much the greater the throng and the
enthusiasm. At Cavillas, two leagues from the
city, their majesties had sent their *officiers de
bouché* to prepare a magnificent banquet. The
French ambassador and ministers of the Crown
received her, but as it was not etiquette for ladies
and gentlemen to eat together, the Princess was
compelled to accept the compliment, but ate in a
room alone. Here was presented to her, by a
courtier who had been sent by the King and Queen,
a letter from the latter, requesting her not to continue her journey, but to await their coming at five
o'clock. The King, the Queen and the whole Court
arrived, the Princess hastened to the door of the
carriage to receive them. They both embraced and
kissed her warmly, displaying before all the assembled
crowd the greatness of their joy. They entered the
house, and went with her to her apartment. On
issuing thence, they pressed her to accompany them
to Madrid in their own carriage. Such an honour
had never before been accorded to any subject, but
Madame des Ursins had the wisdom to refuse, saying
that 'for the first time in her life, she must disobey

her sovereign's commands,' and, entering her own
equipage, she followed the royal carriage to the
town. Slowly, amid the cheers of the people, she
entered Madrid, which she had quitted hardly a year
before in the depths of humiliation and disgrace.
Now, at the summit of her ambition, flushed with
triumph and success, she once more took possession
of the place that had been temporarily lost to her.
That it was an occasion of national rejoicing is a
fact, and a strange one, but still a fact.

While at the French Court, she had all the time
been pulling the strings at Madrid to clear the decks
for political action. Grammont could not contain
himself for fury. He had asked an audience of
the Queen, which she was, of course, unable to
refuse, but her majesty neutralised—or rather reversed—the honour by turning her back upon him.
A system of persecution was begun in order to
drive him to demand his recall; this he soon did,
and was condignly soothed by the application of the
order of the Toison d'Or,—a remedy often applied
by Louis to the wounds inflicted by Madame des
Ursins.

It was just at this time — that of Madame des
Ursins' return to Spain — that all things seemed
to be working together for the ruin of the French
King, and of Philippe, who, of course depended on
his grandfather's fortunes for the success of his own.
But Louis' position had changed very considerably
for the worse since the time when he, as dictator and

arbiter, had imposed his will on Europe. Blenheim
(1704) had cost him not only a fine army, but the
whole of the country that stretched between the
Danube and the Rhine, and the fall of Barcelona in
1705 was a cruel blow, even though by far the
greater part of Spain was on Philippe's side and
showed their loyalty and devotion to the young King,
who unhappily, however, possessed neither generals
nor engineers, and but very few soldiers to follow up
this advantage. In May 1705, the Emperor Leopold
died. The Earl of Peterborough was appointed
by Queen Anne to command the new expedition
against Spain, and was joined by the Archduke
Charles, who was proclaimed king by a band of
revolutionists, and when Barcelona fell before the
onslaughts of Peterborough, Philippe resolved to go
thither in person and strive to reconquer the town.
Setting out from Madrid he joined Tessé, who
was in command of the troops, and marched into
Catalonia at the head of 20,000 men, but, owing to
Tessé's incompetency, reinforcements had entered the
city under Stanhope, and Philippe, through no fault
of his own, had to beat a retreat.

Besides the Queen's grief at her husband's departure,
and fears for his safety, she hated the post of Regent
to which she was nominated during his absence,
although she was unusually capable of filling it.
Madame des Ursins however was now with her and
afforded her some consolation and support, and by
the unflagging energy of both, they succeeded in

raising a few sums of money towards the maintenance
of the troops, and showing a magnificent example of
patience and perseverance under difficulties. Tessé
prosecuted the siege with much want of ability and
decision and entire want of success, and on May
11th the French and Spanish armies were in full
retreat towards the French frontier, leaving the
allied forces in possession of the town. Philippe's
gloomy and superstitious mind was as much
exercised and harassed by the fact that a total
eclipse of the sun darkened the heavens at the
time of their retreat as at the disastrous failure of
their arms.

Uncertain of his destiny, he first retired to
Pampeluna, while Peterborough and the Archduke
were gathering forces in Catalonia. Afterwards he
proceeded to Madrid, where he found the Queen and
Madame des Ursins using every endeavour to support
their failing cause, but the money so urgently needed
was not forthcoming and the Court and the ministry
retreated to Burgos, followed by the Queen and
Madame des Ursins. Philippe joined Berwick's army,
but on June the 25th the allies entered the Spanish
capital, which, though it offered no resistance, accorded
them no welcome, and the absent Archduke was
proclaimed king in the midst of a sullen silence.
Toledo was the home of the Queen-dowager of Spain,
and of its archbishop, Pontocarrero, whose hatred
to Philippe's, or rather to Madame des Ursins' rule,
gathered fresh force at the sight of the apparently

impending fall of the Bourbons. Pontocarrero caused
a solemn *Te Deum* to be performed, illuminated his
palace, and gave a great banquet to celebrate the
entry of the allies into Madrid. Charles remained
at Barcelona, and, in spite of Peterborough's urging
his immediate entry into Madrid, to take possession
of the throne, persisted in dallying so long that a
feeling of resentment, occasioned by his apparent
indifference, broke forth in Castile, where, on the other
hand, Philippe's popularity became suddenly enhanced
in the eyes of the enthusiastic Castillians. Whole
towns rose in his favour; at Toledo the Austrian
standard was torn down, while one of those strange
revulsions of popular feeling that sometimes manifest
themselves in times of political excitement began to
show itself.

The battle of Almanza was fought and gained by
Berwick at this time and changed the course of events ;
the allies found themselves unable to hold Madrid,
and they evacuated the town, which was re-entered
by the Court and the ministry.

In 1707 the Duke of Orleans was sent by Louis to
Spain to join the army ; Berwick was in command,
but the Duke, who had assisted at the siege of Turin,
had by some been accused of being the cause of the
disaster there. He was therefore doubly desirous of
distinguishing himself, but he had first gone to Madrid
and engaged in a preliminary dispute with Madame
des Ursins, whom he made the subject of a low and
indecent jest, and whose enmity he therefore acquired.

A great battle was fought by Berwick, it was a decisive one and it established Philippe more firmly on the throne, but, unfortunately for himself, the Duke of Orleans only arrived the day after. He did not achieve much distinction during the campaign, and when he returned to Madrid his quarrel and dislike to Madame des Ursins were renewed. He had formed a scheme to oust his nephew from the throne, and to take his place upon it. It is said—but it is one of those things that can never be established as a matter of fact—that Louis supported him, and it was thought that it was not possible that France should endure the burden of this war much longer.

In 1709, bowed down by the pressure of his misfortunes, Louis saw no way out of his troubles but to withdraw his protection from Philippe; though to leave him to his own resources pointed to disaster for the young King, even to extinction.

Philippe's flight and abdication were regarded as a certainty, and d'Orleans still hoped to gain the crown for himself. But he was neither prudent in conversation nor judicious in behaviour, considering the importance of his position and the baseness of his intention. All his movements were watched, all his utterances chronicled, and he was, moreover, foolish enough to despise his enemy. After his departure, it is affirmed that complete proof of his guilt was discovered, and the criminal alliance was to be sealed with the House of Austria, by his marriage with the Queen-dowager, the widow of Charles II., d'Orleans

intending to repudiate and put away his own wife,
Louis' natural daughter. It is further affirmed
that to all this the King's ambassador was privy,
but there are some, on the other hand, who assert
that Louis learned with indignation his nephew's
treachery.

At this time the French were beaten everywhere.
Disasters crowded upon them both abroad and at home.
Louis, humiliated and miserable, earnestly desired
peace on even the hardest conditions. He proposed indeed to abandon his grandson. 'It is
impossible,' he wrote to Amelot, 'that we can have
peace so long as he is on the Spanish throne; it
is hard to tell him so, but it must be done.' But
at the Queen's and Madame des Ursins' earnest
representations he had consented to leave twenty-
five battalions in Spain, while twenty-six were to
return to France.

A terrible and humiliating retreat it proved for the
French King. They refused battle with the Aus-
trians twice, though whether the marshal was acting
under orders from his sovereign or not is doubtful.
In Spain, treason was suspected, and Philippe, mortified to the core, sallied forth to command his own
army. It was on such occasions as these that the
Princesse des Ursins showed her mettle; she loved
Spain and was true to the Spanish King and Queen.
She besought Philippe never to abandon his crown,
but rather to perish in the midst of his people. She
believed in the possibility of saving Spain, and that

she could even help France, and events partially justified her words. She had taken a high hand as usual. All officials who had acted under the Archduke's orders, or who had followed his flag, had been exiled. She herself had turned out three hundred ladies, who had refused to follow them to Burgos. Philippe was more generous, and extended pardon to many. He was always kind and hitherto had never forgotten those who served him faithfully.

To peace, even now, Madame des Ursins was passionately opposed, and Madame de Maintenon was equally enthusiastic in its favour. They exchanged letters which bordered on quarrelling : ' Funds are wanting,' said the latter ; ' Funds can be raised,' said the former, ' France is rich and can compass all.' But Madame des Ursins' ascendency, except in Spain, was declining, for Louis, away from the personal influence that was once very potent with him, harassed by anxiety, and overcome with troubles blamed her for many of the complications that had arisen. The correspondence between herself and Madame de Maintenon continued hotly, until at last Madame de Maintenon refused to lay any more of her letters before the King. ' On n'aime pas ici,' she said, ' que les dames s'occupent d'affaires,' an implied accusation which could surely have been answered by Madame des Ursins with a *tu quoque.*

Peace, however, was a necessity, and that of Utrecht was now being formulated. Philippe V. desired to make a condition therein that the Princesse des Ursins should receive a gift of sovereignty in the low countries. This was at first approved by France, but inasmuch as it became a point of difficulty, dispute and procrastination, deferring the conclusion of the treaty, on account of the objections raised by Austria, she became a great source of irritation to those powers who were desirous of peace. She was accused of retarding it for the gratification of her personal ambition. Her great desire was to acquire this sovereignty, and to exchange it for another in Touraine, which would, at her death, return to the crown of France. So certain was she of the success of her plans, that her friend d'Aubigny was already in the act of superintending the building of a magnificent *château* in Touraine, but her second unexpected and final fall extinguished all such hopes.

In 1712 Philippe was settled more firmly on his throne, and the young Queen, eager, generous and impetuous, writes to Madame de Maintenon : ' Je suis assez glorieuse je vous l'avoue pour resentir le plaisir de faire pour ma Camerera-Major, plus que les Reines qui m'ont precedées n'ont fait pour les leurs.' But in 1713 things changed again, and this time the Austrian Emperor, who was apportioned that part of the country which was chosen by the confederates to replace the Bavarian Elector in the Netherlands, declared that no earthly power should make him yield anything to the Princess, his constant, consistent, and persistent enemy, and no modification of other parts of the treaty would induce him to do so.

The earnestly wished-for peace was too precious for
Louis to risk its loss by a fresh quarrel, so the point
was yielded by him, but when the envoy arrived in
Spain from Louis, and brought the treaty for the
Spanish King's final signature, the latter refused to
affix his name unless a clause were inserted to create
the principality. The Marquis de Brancas returned,
indignant and insulted. He declared that Madame
des Ursins ruled all, directed all, and spoilt his
mission. Louis raged, but Philippe persisted in sending his own envoy to remonstrate with his grandfather, while Madame des Ursins plied Madame de
Maintenon with letters. More—by certain diplomatic
actions and words, the English ambassador had engaged that Queen Anne should undertake to secure
this object of the Princess's ambition. Madame des
Ursins endeavoured to decide it by offering to give
up the land at once to Louis, if they would confer it
on her for an equivalent in Touraine. But it was not
to be. During this proceeding, she had, as mentioned,
sent d'Aubigny thither, where she hoped to hold the
position of a sovereign Princess. A small piece of
land was bought in Touraine, and there he began
to build a *château*—the Manoir of Chanteloup. It
was not wise, but England's word had encouraged
her, and with the approval of Holland and of Louis,
and with Madame de Maintenon's support, she fully
expected to get the better of Austria. But England
played her false. The ambassador was blamed for
his undertaking, and the agreement was cancelled.

G

No stone did the uneasy Princess leave unturned for the acquisition of this sovereignty. The negotiations proceeded, but either the negotiators were indiscreet —as she herself was, undoubtedly, in her actions,—or Philippe was injudicious in his ; at anyrate, they failed. The French ministry and Torcy revelled in their revenge, Madame de Maintenon abandoned the sinking ship, and Louis watched the turn that events were taking. 'Sign the treaty,' he said sternly to his grandson, 'or I will withdraw my troops, Spain shall fight her own battles, and I will occupy myself with you no longer. I will not, for the sake of securing the aggrandisement of Madame des Ursins, sacrifice the welfare of my people and plunge France into fresh misfortune.' And no representations or prayers could move him from this position. Philippe signed the peace of Utrecht, as he was, of course, forced to do, without further remonstrance and with no conditions.

Thus were for ever extinguished the life-long hopes and ambitions of the daring and arrogant Princess. Henceforth, although in the immediate future she was to make one more desperate effort to rise and soar above her fellows, failure dogged her footsteps, and she no longer occupied the same position as before.

CHAPTER XII

IT was not long before Philippe was assailed by a
misfortune, the magnitude of which his imagination
never foreshadowed. His true and loyal little wife,
whose energies had been devoted to his interests and
welfare, whose love was as unselfish as it was devoted,
upon whom he had depended for so many years, and
who had borne him three sons, soon after the birth of
her youngest, began to droop and her health to give
way. Very gradual was her decay, and as is so often
the case with the insidious disease of which she died
(consumption), it was long before the full gravity of the
disorder manifested itself either to her or to the on-
lookers. A slight cough, a constantly recurring fever,
loss of appetite and sleep, seemed at first comparatively trivial ailments, with no specific name. But
soon these deceitful symptoms seemed to sap her
strength, and with her daily loss of power, the physicians—very incapable ones—began to feel alarmed.
Philippe, whose love for his wife was the strongest
feeling in his nature, also began to be uneasy. Louise
Marie had been sorely tried in the last few years of
her husband's stormy reign, and it is probable that her
strength had been unequal to the burden laid upon it.
Shortly, all the thousand and one little signs of
anxiety, inseparable from the threatened visit of the
grim king, began to show themselves in the palace.
There exists a letter from Brancas, who writes to

Torcy how that he heard that she slept little, and that her weakness was too great for him to be admitted for an audience. Then follow the sad records of the little ameliorations so eagerly seized upon as indications of real improvement by anxious friends, and the sorrowful return to the original low level. Then a step lower still.

'She was *coiffée*,' he says on one occasion, 'and did not seem so weak as I expected; she had put on a little rouge,' he added, but the cruel fever would not be reduced, and a crisis so alarming occurred that Philippe, who knew not how to exist for his torments of fear, abandoned himself to his grief. He would not quit her room or her side. His alarm was pitiable, his agitation irrepressible, he became wan, thin and ill, but still he would not stir from the side of his beloved. Representations, entreaties were useless, remonstrance unheeded. The physicians became alarmed on his account. Madame des Ursins' appeals failed. The first physician knelt before him, his confessor remonstrated, but Philippe remained, his head sunk on his breast, and made but one answer to his sorrowing subjects, that he would not leave her till she died. Early in February a courier was despatched in frantic haste to the Court of Versailles, taking the following pathetic little note from Philippe to his grandfather :—

'La reine se trouve si reduite en tel état par sa maladie que le besoin de prendre secours est effectif (*sic*). Votre Majesté a tant de bonté pour moi que je ne doute pas qu'elle ne veuille bien y contribuer, ainsi je lui écris en deux mots pour la supplier de m'envoyer Helvétius qu'on dit a de très bons remèdes, avec toute la diligence possible' (*sic*).

Without an instant's delay, Louis despatched the renowned doctor, whose fame was justly great, and the poor little Queen revived a little from the hopes inspired by his expected visit. Relays and relays of horses were sent to meet him, and, if possible, hasten his steps by every imaginable aid to speed. Helvétius had saved the life of the Grand Dauphin, the young King's father, and his skill was deemed unequalled, and poor Philippe, haggard and worn, strove vainly to quell his gnawing anxiety and miserable fears, and to fix his hopes on the great physician's powers. Helvétius was a Dutchman who, in spite of the royal patronage, was subject to the fate of all learned men in advance of their time. He was looked upon by his *confrères* as a quack. He practised according to his own principles, and repudiated those of others, a proceeding which did not enhance his popularity. He was, says St Simon, a good, honest man, patient, charitable, benevolent, with a fund of common-sense and of '*esprit*,' a herald, we may say, of many such another in that noble profession who have pursued their course of enlightened advancement in spite of the disparagement of envious minds. But even Helvétius' genius could not stay the doom that threatened the young Queen—the fiat had gone forth.

He arrived at Madrid on the 12th of February.
Orry had been sent ten leagues to meet him and to
conduct him to the palace. But on the 16th she died,
at eight in the morning. According to his cruel wont,
death had seemed the day before to hesitate a little,
so as to inspire the watchers with some faint hope of
ultimate amelioration. But next morning, she suddenly lost consciousness and died. She had borne
her sufferings with singular patience and endurance.
The King's confessor, Père Robinet, immediately induced Philippe to enter his carriage and drive to the
palace of the Duc de Medina-Coeli, which had been
prepared for the event. Madame des Ursins followed
immediately with the young princes. The grievous
event was sincerely and heartily mourned by all the
people. Her patriotism and devotion, her spirited
efforts to maintain her husband's throne and welfare,
her courage, energy and resolution were long a theme
of admiration and encomium to Philippe's loyal subjects. All her love, all her devotion, all her energies
in life, had been freely lavished on him, and his own
love had never strayed. It was well he mourned her,
for with her died all his happiness. It was fitting he
should bewail her loss, for she was essentially his
better part, the nobler, the more worthy, the more
lofty of purpose. Comparisons are, however, odious,
and Philippe, weak though he was, had been ennobled
by her love and improved by her companionship.

The death of the young Queen did not change
the political aspect of matters. The importance of

Madame des Ursins' position was perhaps temporarily somewhat emphasised. Her influence over Philippe, though great, had found its widest expression through the Queen, and no doubt she realised that some changes must occur which she would have to watch and regulate. Orry, her creature, had been nominated by Philippe a member of the Despacho, an appointment of course originating with herself, not only in order that she should retain the direction of affairs, but to counteract the machinations of Brancas, who was Louis' envoy in the matter of the Treaty of Utrecht, and who kept his master *au courant* of the state of matters at Madrid. He hated Madame des Ursins, and his position at Court had been all along painful and strained.

Philippe, meantime, was overwhelmed with grief. He appeared at first unable to rouse himself from the effects of the blow that had fallen upon him. He would not return to the palace where he had lived so happily with his wife. He shut himself up and refused to see anyone but his children and the Camerera-Major, leading a life of monotonous misery. For a long time no one was permitted to enter his presence, and the influence of Madame des Ursins rose higher and higher, and as time went on, and he was still hidden from the public view, even scandals were not wanting concerning the cause of the extraordinary ascendency that she wielded over the young sovereign. True or false, they seized hold of the public imagination, and it was asserted that a marriage would certainly ensue. Much stress was laid on the fact that a wooden corridor had been erected hastily to unite the King's apartments to those of his children and Madame des Ursins, who inhabited a convent close by. The palace occupied by the King not being large enough for what they required, the monks had been turned out for their accommodation, this giving rise to what it is impossible to help believing was an empty scandal. Still, whether there was the smallest cause, however, for the rumour it is impossible to say. Philippe was so weak a man, and Madame des Ursins so strong and resolute a woman, and her ambition so boundless and illimitable, that one cannot help thinking it just possible that she may have aspired to be Queen. It is certain that she encouraged his gloom and desire for seclusion, and rumours without end flew about the town. It was positively asserted that she intended to marry the King, and the report spread, — reached France, — reached Madame de Maintenon,—reached Louis.

Extremes of feeling seldom endure long, and as time advanced, Philippe wearied of the restraint. She had permitted him latterly to see a chosen few companions, who reported him to be willing to be amused and interested. Someone amongst these found an opportunity of conveying to him the stories that were afloat concerning the relations of himself and the Princess, and one of the most daring told him that it was rumoured he thought of marrying her. Philippe paused and became very red. '*Oh, pour*

marier non !' said he angrily, unconsciously echoing
the very words that had before played a conspicuous
part in the Princess's story. He was saved however.

It is recorded that a young and beautiful lady was
at this time introduced to the Court, one whom his
rank forbade him to marry, and it was clear that
Madame des Ursins, dreading the influence of a wife,
desired that he should form a more equivocal *liaison*.
His life, however, was perfectly pure—he was singularly desirous of leading a chaste life. But still the
Camerera-Major's influence was checked, for the report had irritated him. 'Cherchez moi une femme,'
said Philippe angrily, in the first words of command
or implied censure that he had ever spoken to her.

The commission was a death-blow to her unde-
fined hopes and defined fears, for whether or no she
believed that he was capable of committing such an
act of almost insane folly as that which she is supposed to have desired, she had unquestionably wished
to postpone such an event as marriage with another,
the result of which must be fraught with such uncertain results to herself. But Philippe had spoken, and
instinctively she knew that in this case there was no
appeal. Still things are never in so sorry a plight
but that they may be worse, and at least the choice
lay with *her*, although it was not likely that she
would find such another treasure as the good and
true little Savoyarde, who had proved such a loving
wife, such a loyal and eager follower, such an affectionate coadjutor.

CHAPTER XIII

AT this.time Parma was governed by a Duke who, having no children, had adopted a niece with the intention of her succeeding to the Dukedoms of Parma, etc. The Abbé Alberoni, at this time a man of considerable influence in Madrid, had been several times employed in ecclesiastical missions. He was a man of great acuteness and subtlety, and the Duc de Vendôme had, during his campaigns in Spain, attached him to his person as almoner, and he was now in the service of the Parmesan minister at Madrid. He was highly ambitious, and on friendly terms with the Grand Inquisitor, Cardinal Giudice. He insinuated himself into his intimacy as he did into that of Madame des Ursins, and, seeing the advancement and distinction that would accrue to him did the young Princess Elizabeth Farnese fill the important vacant post, he resolved to do all in his power to bring about the alliance. Profound in diplomacy, ambitious, unscrupulous, self-reliant, Madame des Ursins' craftiness of character contained that curious lapse which is so often apparent in persons of a like nature. She believed herself to be undupeable, although she was a child in the cunning hands of the wily priest. 'On peut être plus fin que les autres, mais non pas que tous les autres' is an assertion of an acute and refined contemporary, and she would have done well to remember the axiom. She had no suspicions of the secret and ambitious design that was being hatched in the teeming brain of the Jesuit. The plot had been mooted at Versailles; it would have been a blow to her vanity had she believed that she played only a second part in the suggestion, and that her appearance on the scene was the result of the most artful manipulation. Who knew better than Alberoni the qualities—to which political ones were as nought—that were, in the Princess's eyes, indispensable for the Queen of Spain? The picture he drew of the young Princess was as false to her nature as it was well adapted to Madame des Ursins' wishes, and as it was ill-adapted to truth. Gentleness, said Alberoni, tact, modesty, and submissiveness were her characteristics, and of qualities to adorn a queen she was full; pliable and easily led, he added, there was nothing left to desire.

All this Madame des Ursins heard and accepted, and she resolved that Elizabeth Farnese and no other should marry the King of Spain. Alberoni was at once despatched to Parma to commence negotiations. Things promised well. Alberoni returned, bringing a favourable reply. She interviewed him, inquired, probed, and was assured by him that all was well. Still she was not *quite* satisfied. She feared she might not find Elizabeth as humble and docile a pupil as she desired. But her industrious and untiring efforts to compass her designs were unceasing, though in this case, as in others, some one conspicuous element to ensure success must have been wanting in her. She

was too bold, too secure of her own judgment and
powers, though Alberoni assured her solemnly that
Elizabeth was possessed of every quality that was
conspicuous by its absence; but what was more natural
than to believe that one brought up in the small and
insignificant Court of Parma, unaccustomed to the
ways of the world, would be only too grateful to be
provided with so splendid a destiny? So Alberoni
drew Madame des Ursins into his net, and was instrumental in bringing about the marriage fraught
with such dire consequences to the latter. His active ambition resolved that he would oust her and
take her place. It is really curious that one so astute
as the Princess should have been so easily misled.
Philippe himself was quite ready to accept any wife
that was offered to him; and so, on the interested
and unreliable assurances of Alberoni, Madame des
Ursins caused the necessary overtures to be made,
and the preliminaries were duly arranged. At the
very last moment it was whispered in the Princess's
ear that the bride by no means answered the alluring
descriptions of the artful Alberoni. We are not told
through whom the discovery was made, but the effect
on Madame des Ursins was so startling that she
waited neither confirmation nor denial of the alleged
facts. She instantly despatched a courier to stop all
the marriage preparations at Parma. The messenger,
however, only arrived the morning of the very day
on which the wedding was to be celebrated by proxy,
bearing despatches to postpone the ceremony. No

sooner were those alarming instructions perused by
the uncle and niece than they resolved to clinch the
matter then and there, rather than trust to the perilous contingencies of postponement and re-arrange-
ment. The unhappy courier was seized and threatened
with instant death if he refused to consent to the
alternative they offered him, namely, one day's im-
prisonment and a gift of a sum of money. The
marriage ceremony was to be performed during his
incarceration, and, when he issued from prison, he
was to feign having just arrived. Of course, the
alternative was gladly accepted, and the wedding
duly solemnised, another special messenger being despatched to inform the Spanish monarch of the conclusion of the wedding, as well as of the bride having
actually started on her journey to meet him. It is
easy to believe that the above episode did not tend
to mitigate Elizabeth's fell intentions towards the
Camerera-Major, whose pretensions she had from the
first resented bitterly and whom she resolved to eject.
It is uncertain whether, in the summary proceedings
that followed, Alberoni was, or was not, a conspirator
and participator. Our own opinion is that he was.
However, St Simon says, he met the bride at Pampeluna, one of the halting-places on the line of her journey, and had a long interview with her; that she then
informed him of her intentions of ejecting the Princess
from her presence on the spot, and that he remonstrated and advised her against so audacious a proceeding. He found her agitated and irritated, pacing

the small room angrily, and vowing vengeance against
the Camerera; that he expostulated, telling her that
she would incur the King's serious displeasure, but that
she then produced a letter from her husband author-
ising her to act as she pleased, and so she continued
her journey, panting for the revenge which she overtook and carried out.

Alberoni's character was so deceitful that it is probable he knew by thus remonstrating he was ensuring
the fate of the doomed Camerera, but he was simply
covering his own part in the transaction by taking the
best means—that of opposition—to make the Queen
effect what he himself ardently desired. She would
thus incur the whole responsibility, although he apparently used all his powers to check her action,
while she passionately answered that she would do as
seemed best to herself, and would carry out her purpose. 'Silence!' she said, when Alberoni pretended
to impress on her the rashness of such a proceeding,
and she immediately afterwards pursued her journey.

Meantime Philippe was, of course, wholly unaware
of the manœuvre that had been practised to try to
stop the marriage, and he arrived at the little town of
Guadalaxara, where the meeting between himself and
his bride had been agreed upon. Madame des Ursins,
equally ignorant of what had happened at Parma,
save that her courier had not arrived in time to arrest
the marriage, resolved to put a good face on the matter
and ignore all, save the festive occasion of their meeting. The marriage was to be finally celebrated at

Guadalaxara, in a private chapel of great beauty belonging to one of the grandees. The Princess seems to have accompanied Philippe to this point, and then to have left him and gone on before to meet the *fiancée*. It was the 22d of December, the roads were bad, and the weather bitterly inclement. Accompanied by a very few retainers she reached Quadraque, where the young Queen was to rest that night. On her arrival she was informed that her majesty was already there, and had alighted at a small lodging which had been prepared for her—the best the town afforded. It was exactly opposite to that at which the Princess descended. The latter had journeyed from Guadalaxara, and had left the King's presence in full Court costume. After halting to add a few touches to her toilette, she crossed the road and entered the Queen's abode.

Elizabeth Farnese's life had been passed, if not in seclusion, at any rate in comparative retirement; a condition of things which did not prevent her from carrying out her resolution relentlessly. The attendants left them alone. The tyro surveyed the veteran of seventy-two with aggressive haughtiness, not to say rudeness, while the latter began to comprehend that the interview was not to be a pacific one. One account states, that Madame des Ursins informed her majesty that her dress was not in accordance with the usage of Spanish etiquette, and Duclos avers, that the Princess's criticism so exasperated the newly-fledged Queen that she retorted that she was surprised the Princess ventured into her presence. All the attendants were outside, and had left the little chamber so eminently unfitted to be a battle-field for the angry belligerents. They faced each other, the one in the pride of her insolent youth —untaught, arrogant, insulting, audacious; the other, from the height of her superiority—calm, dignified, imposing, sagacious; the former undaunted by her opponent's powerful presence; the latter regarding her antagonist as the girl presumptuously faced her with judicious calmness, not once abandoning the respect due to her rank, but dealing with her in some sort as a refractory child. She tendered such apologies as she considered due to the Queen, who, so far from becoming calmer, reattacked her for appearing in a dress she deemed unfitting, and finished by loudly calling out for help from the attacks of a madwoman. In vain did the Princess assure her of her respect, and of her innocence of any intentional offence. The more she said, so much the louder did the Queen shriek for aid, calling on the officers of her guard that she was threatened by a lunatic who was insulting her, and whom she required them to eject. Taking no notice of Madame des Ursins' protestations, the Queen actually caused to be effected what she required, and seizing her by the shoulders, the lieutenant commanding the escort removed her from her majesty's presence. She commanded her own *écuyer*, who, hearing the clatter had followed the lieutenant into the chamber to arrest Madame des

Ursins, and not to leave his hold of her until he placed her in her carriage with two other officers in charge of her person, and fifteen soldiers to surround the equipage. She ordered six horses to be procured, and within an hour, in accordance with the impatient and arrogant instructions of the young Queen, Madame des Ursins was *en route* to Bayonne, with commands that there was to be neither delay nor halt. The lieutenant, alarmed and confused, had stammered that the King alone could give such an order. ' Have you not one,' said the Queen haughtily, ' wherein he instructs you to obey me without remonstrance?' And indeed the officer did possess such a document, and so he dared not disobey, although the army had been in the habit of treating the Princess with the same awe and respect as that due to the King himself.

The ground was white with snow and frost, and Madame des Ursins, unable to realise, hardly even to comprehend the gist of such extraordinary commands, unprepared with any provisions of extra clothing or comforts to protect her from the inclemency of the weather, scarcely credited the extremity of the revenge to which she was about to be subjected. She persuaded an attendant to convey a message to the Queen asking an audience of her majesty, but the latter only displayed an almost insane fury that such a liberty should have been taken, and that her commands had not been already complied with. At seven at night, the ground being slippery with ice and the weather bitterly cold, with no more protection

H

against it than she had brought with her from Guadalaxara, the Princess and two officers entered the
carriage, and, surrounded by a guard of soldiers,
drove forth into outer darkness. Who can depict
the condition, physical and mental, of the unhappy
woman on this cruel December night — insulted,
deserted, vanquished? Was ever fall so sudden and
precipitous, so humiliating and complete, and that,
too, by the act of an insignificant little upstart, whose
words were only not pert, because they were insolent; her behaviour only not ridiculous, because its
effects were dire and tragic? That it should be in
the power of such an one to heap indignities upon
her! For, whatever her own audacity, it was at least
that of a giant before that of a dwarf. Whatever her
errors, and they had been neither few nor venial, whatever her presumption, and it had been great, the
punishment she merited was not this — the shrill,
malapert, ill-bred, contumelious spite of a mere child.

Can it be believed that for more than a fortnight this
horrible journey was continued with only such relief
and mitigation of its hardships as could be afforded at
the small villages through which their large, cumbrous,
uneasy, jolting carriage laboured on its way to St Jean
de Luz, the little frontier town? The cold was so intense that it is said the driver's hands were frost-
bitten, the food so bad as to be almost uneatable and
to necessitate her living on eggs. And so she journeyed on, expecting each moment to see a horseman
pursuing the carriage, a messenger from Philippe, who

she did not doubt, would avenge these horrible insults.
But no one came, and she learned at last that she
was indeed ruined, abandoned, and that the term of
her power had been reached. Till she got to St Jean
de Luz, she was actually unable to change her clothes.
What epithet is strong enough to describe the cruelty
of such conduct, even if it were due to the passive
permission of one who had profited by her intellect, and
had been guided by her capacities? As time advanced,
and she realised the truth, the spirit of the insulted,
resolute, and courageous woman rose. She would
show no weakness, even if death were the result. She
braced herself during that endless and terrible journey
to face the humiliation of her new position, and if
indignant and wounded, she was yet silent—uncom-
plaining, if insulted.—Her two nephews, Lanti and de
Chalais, had been permitted to follow her, and she
learned from them the truth that she must accept the
position, which was endorsed by the Spanish King.
Neither word, tear, nor sigh escaped her, as she pursued her journey and finished it in this destitute and
painful condition. When she arrived at St Jean de
Luz, she lay down for the first time for twenty days
on a bed, and obtained proper food and clothing.
Never was the destruction and downfall of an enemy
so cruelly and deliberately planned, or carried out
with a vengeance so harsh and unrelenting. But
though persecuted, she was not overwhelmed ; though
vanquished by brute force, her intellect was not
crushed, and on her arrival at St Jean de Luz, she in-

stantly despatched a messenger to the French King, shortly describing the shameful story, and asking permission to go to Versailles to lay the facts, *de vive voix*, before him. She also wrote the history of these events to Madame de Maintenon, setting forth the insults she had received, with much dignity. In truth, it was in adversity that this extraordinary woman rose to the full height of her merits. She had, she said, been treated, in the face of Europe, by the Queen of Spain, as if she were the meanest and most degraded of wretches,—she, who had been for years honoured by the confidence of the greatest monarchs on earth. She refused to believe that the King of Spain was privy to these indignities and cruelties. She had sent her nephew to Madrid to lay it all before him, and he had orders to go on to Versailles, for she had too high an opinion of Madame de Maintenon to believe otherwise than that she would be admitted to her presence. Meanwhile, she would await the King's orders at St Jean de Luz, in a little house by the seaside. 'Her enemies were rising up against her,' she said.

Many people said that she was the victim of her own enmity to, and attacks upon, the Inquisition, for Louis had not approved the decided part she had taken against this ancient and popular institution. The whole of the French Court now clamoured against her; while Madame de Maintenon wrote,—'Nous trouvons Orry point à sa place, et Espagne assez mal gouvernée par Madame des Ursins.' Torcy and all

her old friends, many of whom had climbed to distinction through her, all were against her, but she
clung to Louis, as she had every right to do, and
believed in his protection.

————

CHAPTER XIV

TURN we now to Philippe, whom we left impatiently
awaiting his bride at Guadalaxara. A messenger
soon arrived with a letter from Elizabeth, narrating
the events which had taken place at Quadraque, and
an answer was written by the King, and despatched by
the same messenger to her. Philippe kept his own
counsel and spoke no word, and the courier was so
closely kept by him and the reply so expeditiously
returned, that the latter could not impart the wonder-
ful intelligence. The news, however—as all news
will—leaped out next morning, to the wonderment,
excitement, and curiosity of the courtiers. Many
were the speculations as to what the King's reply
could have conveyed, but no one dared inquire,
though it was the general belief that the Princesse des
Ursins' day was wearing to a close. Lanti and
Chalais, to their honour, braved his anger, and asked
leave to follow, accompany, and escort their fallen
kinswoman to her exile. To this request, the King
gladly consented, charging them with a letter from
himself to the Princess in which he told her that, deeply
as he regretted what had passed, he was unable to

interpose his authority to prevent the Queen having her way; ending by assuring her that all her pensions would be continued, and that he himself would see that they were punctually paid—a promise which he fulfilled to the letter until she died.

The Queen arrived in due time at Guadalaxara, and the marriage between her and the King was at once solemnised. No one ever knew what passed between them on the subject of the fallen Camerera-Major. Every appointment which had been made by her in the new household of the Queen held good, to the enormous relief of those who composed it, and who were shaking in their shoes, from fear that their own fall should coincide with hers. The next day the King and Queen left for Madrid, where they duly arrived,—and thus the Princesse des Ursins, with her fourteen years of despotism, of arbitrary procedure, of arrogant and overbearing tyranny, became a story of the past.

It was not, however, given to Madame des Ursins, any more than to other fallen heroine, to realise that her *rôle* was finished—her part played out—that the curtain was about to fall on the fifth act of the drama.—It was coming to pass that her presence would have been an obstacle instead of a service, and her later actions had been unutterably unwise. That she should have openly interfered with the conditions of the Peace of Utrecht, interposing, as it were, her own person in opposition to its fulfilment, was worse than a crime— it was a blunder. Indeed, it was both—but it was the blunder which doomed the edifice, so carefully reared, so painfully watched, so desperately supported. Her task was done—and with the last touch, like every house of cards, it had fallen. It was impossible to erect another. Philippe always had been—always would be—led by and through his wife, and the *pâte* of the termagant Queen was of another kind to that of the loyal, affectionate, and intelligent little Savoyarde, whose only object during her short life had been to serve those she loved so deeply and truly. Madame de Maintenon wrote to Madame des Ursins inviting her to Versailles. Her nephew had been graciously received there, and Louis had expressed himself kindly concerning her. But the French King was at this time nearing his end. The last few years had been to him tragic in the extreme. Such misfortunes as had darkened them, although they had not crushed his kingly spirit, had sapped his physical strength. He had seen his son, his grandson, and his cherished granddaughter—the last mentioned, the wife of the Duke of Burgundy—yield up their lives in a manner so sudden and terrible, that if the mention of poison were avoided in the royal circle, it was because it was well-known that the discovery of the perpetrator would be appalling—horrible—fearful,—too horrible, indeed, for even the suspicion to be mentioned; and Louis lived on for a short time under the shadow of these awful possibilities.

Accepting the permission she had received to go to Versailles, the Princess put herself in communication with Madrid, for Orry, who was still there in the capacity of minister, remained her firm friend, the only one left! In short, her following was destroyed, and her hopes shattered, for a new *régime* obtained in the Spanish capital. The Queen-dowager had been sent to her own country, and the Grand Inquisitor had received the Portfolio of Foreign Affairs. All Madame des Ursins' system was displaced, and nothing was wanting to show the determination of both King and Queen to wipe out all remembrance of her authoritative reign. But still she clung to the hope of a restoration. A letter to Orry contains words which prove that though cast down she anticipated rising again :—'Il faut prendre patience,' she says, 'jusqu'à ce que j'ai un peu démêlé les choses, et que je sois mise au fait de tout ceci.' She either would not believe in her defeat, or was too proud to acknowledge it—we think the latter. She went to Paris, to her brother, the Duc de Noirmoustier. He was kind to her in her sorrow, as was her old friend, Madame de Noailles. But at Versailles her influence was gone. The King was visibly sinking into his grave, and d'Orleans, her bitter and relentless foe, was already worshipped as the rising sun. Louis himself had hardly been more flattered, more pursued, more surrounded by courtiers, than was the future Regent at this time. He hated Madame des Ursins, and was extremely reluctant that she should approach Versailles, and it was with considerable difficulty that she at length accomplished her purpose. Madame de Maintenon made no sign, and d'Orleans and his wife and mother requested that she should not enter into any of their apartments, and exacted the same from all their entourage. Madame des Ursins must have remembered with bitterness the day when she stood there on an exalted pinnacle, when the King paid her his courtly attentions, and when she was, for a short time, deemed hardly second in importance even to Madame de Maintenon.

It was with considerable difficulty that St Simon, who had been on terms of intimate friendship with her, obtained the permission, without which he dared not act, to visit her, a favour that was only granted on certain conditions.

He describes the interview as having been friendly and frank. She recounted the full history of her misfortunes, speaking, however, in the highest terms of Philippe himself. She hid nothing of the surprise, or of the gross and deliberately planned insults to which she had been subjected,—her departure in evening dress,—the terrible journey,—and all the miseries that she had endured. She spoke of the late Queen, of Philippe, and of many who had figured at Madrid with her, and of the present difficulties of an honourable retreat—whither, she knew not. For eight hours, said St Simon, which appeared no more than so many minutes, he conversed with her, only parting from her after many promises that she would announce to him the day of her departure, so that he should see her once more.

Her stay at Versailles was miserable. Once she

dined with the Duchesse de Lude who belonged to the Court, and once more she was permitted to await the King in the apartment of Madame de Maintenon. But she was not alone with him, and she retired afterwards to the house of the wife of a clerk in an office, where she supped and slept. Next day she dined with Madame de Ventadour, and returned to Paris. She gave up her pension in consideration of receiving some rents from the Hôtel de Ville, and thus obtained 40,000 francs, a sum she well knew she would lose when the Duc d'Orleans came into power. She meditated retiring to Holland, but the États Généraux refused to permit her to enter Amsterdam or the Hague. She then directed her thoughts towards Italy, and returned only to take leave of the Court.

Madame des Ursins hoped that the Spanish King might bestow upon her, besides the pensions, some mark of his recognition of former services, but he was, of course, entirely under the dominion of his revengeful and venomous wife, and no additional favour was granted. Louis, however, had desired this should be effected, for he was never unmindful of services rendered. But he was old and unpersistent, forgetful and feeble, and Madame de Maintenon, smarting with the recollection of recent epistolary encounters, did not take the matter up. Madame des Ursins was cut to the quick. She could not refrain from speaking her mind to her quondam friend, Mme. de Noailles :—

' J'ai prié,' she says, ' M. de Villeroi de vous faire

lecteur d'une lettre du Roi d'Espagne, refusant de
suivre à mon égard l'exemple de Louis Quatorze qui
lui conseillait de le faire. Ce refus bien qu'une telle
réponse lui a été inspirée, madame, car il est trop con-
traire a sa générosité (*sic*). Pour surcroît de douleurs
j'ai mis mes yeux entre les mains de M. de St Yves.
Perdre mes yeux et ma faveur ce serait trop de
malheur à la fois ! Mais, quoiqu'il arrive, croyez-le
bien, le reste de ma vie sera employé à prier Dieu pour
le Roi, mon bienfaiteur, et pour vous, madame. Quelle
destinée est la mienne ! Chassée d'Espagne avec indig-
nité, acceuillie avec bonté par le Roi dont je suis la
sujette, privée néanmoins encore de la consolation
de le voir en particulier, je suis en outre pressée
par mes amis de sortir de son royaume comme
si ma présence l'embarrassait. Le Roi, me disent-ils
se charge d'obtenir de la Court le consentement a ce
que je me retire chez moi a Rome. Parlez, madame.
Auriez-vous cru, lorsque vous me conseilliez de ne pas
quitter Madrid que je ne trouverais pas un lieu pour y
mettre le pied ? Que de choses là-dessus pourrais-je
dire que la prudence veut que j'étouffe ! '

Misfortunes never come singly. The condition of
the King's health was but too apparent, he was sinking
surely away. She knew she had nothing but persecutions to expect when he was gone. She could
not face what was coming. Not knowing where to
turn, she asked permission to go to Marly to take
leave of the King. Surreptitiously St Simon contrived to meet her. 'She came,' says he, 'on the

6th of August. She had planned it so as to arrive when
the King was coming away from dinner about two
o'clock. She was admitted to his private room, where
she remained alone for half an hour or more with him.
On leaving him, she went to Madame de Maintenon's,
with whom she stayed for an hour. From thence she
immediately drove back to Paris. I had contrived
that I should meet her, and, just as I was inquiring of
her servants where she was, she came out.' She made
him enter the carriage with her, and they were
together for nearly an hour. She concealed from him
none of her fears for the future, nor the blank she
found at the Court and even at Paris, nor yet her
doubt as to where she should take up her abode. The
coldness of the King was apparent even though he
was most courteous. All—all she told St Simon
in every detail, uttering no words of complaint or
regret, and displaying no feebleness. She was composed in manner and measured in speech, talking of
her own affairs precisely as if they were those of
another, and apparently superior to whatever should
result. She alluded, in passing, to Spanish affairs, re-
marking lightly on the power and influence the Queen
was every day acquiring over her husband, adding
that that could never have been otherwise. What St
Simon replied to these confidences he never told.
He at once confessed the interview to the 'rising sun,'
and we have no doubt that he was aware beforehand
that he could make his excuses satisfactorily, together
with his peace with the Duke.

CHAPTER XV

MADAME DES URSINS left Paris on the 14th of August 1715, escorted by her nephews. The Hague, as we have said, and Amsterdam refused to give her hospitality. She hated returning to Rome, where she had been so well known, and, indeed,. she knew not what kind of reception she would meet there. Fifteen years of absence make great changes. Her future was gloomy and desolate indeed. She had not journeyed far before rumours reached her that the King of France was *in extremis*. Fearful of finding herself on French soil at the time of his death, and in the power of her enemy d'Orleans, she flew to Chambéry as the nearest place of security, where she halted. On her arrival, she heard that the end had come, and that Louis' magnificent reign, which had latterly been so clouded and darkened, so threatening and so sorrowful, was closed. Madame de Maintenon, with whom she still appeared to keep up the semblance of friendship, wrote to her on September 11th :—'Il faut baisser la tête sous la main qui nous frappe.' She wrote from St Cyr, whither she had retreated in pious haste when poor Louis was struggling with death :—'Je voudrais,' she continues, 'que votre état fut aussi heureux que le mien. J'ai vu mourir le Roi comme un saint, et comme un héros. J'ai quitté le monde que je n'aimais pas ; je suis dans la plus paisible retraite.' Were Madame de Maintenon our heroine, and not Madame des Ursins, we would observe that this description was an undue development of her imagination, inasmuch as she carefully avoided being with Louis during his passage through the valley of the shadow of death ; and this assurance of her own contentment was a strong contrast to the feelings of Madame des Ursins, who replied, somewhat ironically, that she participated in her admiration for so beautiful and edifying a death, but 'Moi,' she said bitterly, 'J'ignore encore où je pourrai mourir.'

At length she thought she would go to Geneva. Here she remained for a few years, but she wearied of its dulness. She could not exist without movement, and life and intrigue. At Geneva there were none. She was not made much of, and she turned her thoughts towards Rome, and approached her brother, the cardinal, endeavouring to discover what would be her position if she returned. France and Spain were importantly represented there, while the Regent and his cousin were fulfilling the prophecy that had been so bitterly made by Madame des Ursins, and were at open war the one with the other. Philippe—perhaps his conscience somewhat pricked him when he thought of the unchivalrous way in which he had treated his old friend,—took measures to assure her that her fears concerning the manner of her reception at Rome by his envoy were groundless. The Marquis de St Philippe, Ambassador from Spain to Geneva, was charged to assure her of these soothing tidings. This was in 1718. She corresponded with Orry, the only one left of her followers, and wrote to him, in terms of gratitude, that Philippe had sent his ambassador to assure her of his continued esteem, his friendship and protection, and that wherever she went, his ministers would have instructions to make these sentiments known. She wrote in extraordinary terms of gratitude for so mitigated a favour, but Philippe must have had many qualms, as at the same time he added to her pension.

When she went to Rome, the Pope received her with kindness and consideration. She attached herself to the Court of the Stuarts, which was established there, in mitigated grandeur; but she was rich, and she was at a Court, and thus was not unhappy. She was considered highly by some, and very little by others. She was energetic, witty, lively, and she preserved all these qualities till she died. Agreeable, and in a sense still young, she expired at the age of eighty after a very short illness.

CHAPTER XVI

THERE is a curious similarity between the careers of Madame des Ursins and Madame de Maintenon, but their characters were widely different. Each was absorbed in the subjugation and guidance of her own king, and each compassed her end after her own fashion. Madame des Ursins, irascible, impetuous, eager, irrepressible and frank ; Madame de Maintenon

less bold, more subtle, and more patient, calm and
deliberate.   Madame des Ursins was in no wise
dévote, and we may add that between the lines of
her letters we read a kind of contemptuous toleration
of her friend's weakness in this direction.   The latter
served both God and Mammon with equal zest, but
we believe that, this notwithstanding, her religion
was absolutely sincere, or, at anyrate, she believed it
was.   And between those two conditions, who shall
discriminate?   Madame des Ursins was never cast
down.   Defeat only spurred her on to fresh efforts,
and but for these, Spain and Philippe would not have
emerged from their difficulties.   Madame de Maintenon, on the other hand, ruled quietly, though calmly,
and absolutely.   Her motto was '*L'homme propose,
mais Dieu dispose,*' and when this was illustrated, she
submitted and prayed.   That of Madame des Ursins
was '*Aides-toi, et Dieu t'aidera,*' and to this energetic
creed she was constantly faithful.   Their mutual
relations form an interesting picture of the politics
of the times, and some of the letters which passed
betweeen them are admirable specimens of the
epistles of the day.   Madame des Ursins' flow hot
from her pen ; there is no hesitation in her decisive
words, though there are often anger, irony, and sometimes indignation, which at times savoured so much
of sincerity as to be indiscreet.

Although we might perhaps shrink from welcoming a Madame des Ursins at the corner of our
domestic hearth, we regret that the species is extinct

—is a thing of the past—and that we shall witness on the world's public stage such inspiriting and energetic characters no more for ever.

That hers was one of unmitigated restless ambition is true, that she was quite unscrupulous, and in many cases double-dealing in her actions may be admitted, but she never swerved from her allegiance to Spain since the hour that she, seeking hither and thither for a field for her talents, placed them at the disposition of that country, then tottering in its enervated condition to its very base. She followed the fortunes of the young King, as we know, and although in many instances she displayed selfish and mercenary qualities, yet Spain and Philippe owed her much. Both weak, both almost powerless, each was indebted to her masculine resolution for many a result that could neither have been originated or carried out without her. So the disgraceful manner of her dismissal, and the ignominy of her fall, echo to us through the ages, a shameful instance of services unrequited and benefits forgot.

I

ANDRÉ

ANDRE

———o———

LITTLE more than one hundred years ago, when America, stung to the quick by the tyrannical oppression and fanaticism of British statesmen asserted her independence and flew to arms to enforce her will, there occurred an interlude which might have passed by without much notice but for the military rank and interesting character of the principal actor in the drama, which gave unusual prominence to an incident not otherwise uncommon on the theatre of war. No one but those connected by family or professional ties with John André knew anything about him before his name was surrounded by the halo that now encircles it, and although he was a man of unusual merit, it is likely that but for this event his name would not have been known beyond the circle of his own immediate friends and comrades, but it is desirable, before recounting the tragic story of his death, to give a short sketch of his early life.

He was born in London in 1751, his father came of a respectable Swiss family, and had migrated to

England, there to push his fortune. He was fairly
successful in his enterprises, he was a merchant in
London, and he sent his eldest son, John, to Geneva
to be educated, intending that he should follow the
same career.

Young André, however, returned to his father's house
with very different aspirations, he evinced a strong
dislike to the mercantile profession, and earnestly
entreated his father to permit him to enter the army.
He was a bright, eager, spirited boy, but in those days
parental authority was more rigorously enforced than
in these, and he was obliged to submit to the paternal
decree. He had made the most of his education at
Geneva, was an excellent linguist, an adept in the
school of military design, and a proficient in poetry,
music and painting. It cannot then be subject for
wonder that one possessed of so many and rare gifts,
should demur at the dull and uncongenial occupation
prepared for him. His father, however, remained
obdurate, but in spite of this difference of views their
relations were perfectly harmonious, nor did young
André cease to plead for the gratification of his heart's
desire.

But while he was still driving his quill and urging
his cause his father died suddenly, leaving him the
sole protector and guardian of his mother and sisters.
André entered upon his new and onerous duties with
a full sense of their responsibilities, but in his heart
he still cherished his darling ambition. Before long,
he transported his mother and sisters into Derbyshire,

where he hoped the change of scene might mitigate their grief. While staying at Buxton, they made the acquaintance of Miss Seward of Litchfield. She was an intellectual and agreeable woman—it was rare in those days to meet a lady of so comprehensive and cultivated a mind,—and it was a new experience in young André's life which had latterly been spent in the wearisome and distasteful occupation assigned to him, to associate with one so accomplished and appreciative. Litchfield—the birthplace of Johnson —was held high in repute in the literary world, and Miss Seward reigned supreme over a classic coterie, of which André speedily became a leading member, acquiring considerable reputation for literary and artistic merit, and thus it was that a pleasant companionship and a warm friendship ensued. In Miss Seward's house lived a very beautiful young lady, the daughter of a widowed Staffordshire gentleman. At her own mother's death, she had been adopted by Miss Seward—and now the *sequiter* was inevitable; and André, young, handsome and chivalrous as a youthful knight of romance, fell desperately in love with the beautiful Honora Sneyd, whose devotion seemed at first little less ardent than his own. Miss Seward, who was a lady of a certain age and lived in an atmosphere of romance, encouraged the attachment without much regard to the chances of a successful issue. The betrothal was mooted, but as the means of subsistence were of the slenderest, the engagement was, probably by Honora's father, prohibited, seeing that it

would necessarily involve an engagement of indefinite
length, and a long separation. André's love was strong
enough to face any contingency, could he but see any
chance of winning Honora ultimately, and he pleaded
his cause with all the fervency of his youthful enthusiasm and ardent passion ; Honora, however, seems to
have yielded more willingly to the will of her father,
while André determined to persevere in his endeavours to overcome the obstacles to his happiness—and
Miss Seward, eager to secure him the object of his
affections, induced him to return to London and
apply himself to business, while a correspondence
with herself and a rare visit to Litchfield were his
only consolations during this unsatisfactory state of
things.   In spite however of all his sighs it became
clear to himself that his influence with Honora was
declining, and a very few months saw him shifted
from the position of a lover to that of a friend.   To
André's warm and impetuous nature this change was
intolerable, and so long as he saw the least chance of
regaining his old place in her affections he pursued
his work in the counting-house and continued his
periodical visits to Litchfield, refusing to relinquish
the forlorn hope that he might win a sufficient compe-
tency to warrant his suit.   But it was not to be, she
encouraged the attentions of others, and André at
length realised the truth ; thus, by degrees, his visits
ceased, and the correspondence—which occasionally
included a letter to Honora—came to an end.

Some of Honora's suitors—at anyrate, two of them

—were provided with the means, the lack of which was poor André's only defect. Mr Day—of *Sandford and Merton* notoriety,—enveloped in the self-complacency with which the unaccountable success of that inflated production surrounded him, delegated his friend and colleague, Richard Lovell Edgworth, with more credulity than caution, to woo the lovely Honora on commission. Rashly, though at first quite guilelessly, Mr Edgworth undertook the task, and promptly fell in love with her himself—but being unluckily, married, he fled her presence, leaving poor, prosy, pompous Day to the prosecution of his own gallantries. Honora, of course, refused the pedant, and Edgworth's wife dying soon after, he returned to the charge on his own account, urged his own cause, and finally married her. He had large estates in Ireland, whither they retired and lived very happy till 1780, when Honora died of consumption, five months before André suffered at Tappan.

When André became convinced that his hopes would not be fulfilled, his heart turned back towards his old ambition, and a soldier's career presented itself to his vivid imagination with greater attractions than ever. Although he was destitute of influential connections, he managed to procure a commission in the 24th Fusileers, and received orders to join his regiment in America in 1774. Before departing, he travelled to Litchfield to say farewell to his old friends, and once more to look upon the scenes of his happiness. It is in connection with this visit that

a story is told which, being well authenticated, may
find a place here.

In the vicinity of Litchfield lived a gentleman, a
friend of Miss Seward, who had expressed a wish
to become acquainted with one of whom that lady
always spoke so enthusiastically ; it had, therefore,
been arranged that during this, his farewell visit, she
should go with André to Mr Cunningham's house in
order to present him.

On the morning of the appointed day, Mr Cunningham awaited their arrival in company with a friend.
'It is curious,' he said to the latter, a Mr Newton,
'that I have been most unreasonably disturbed by a
dream I had last night, and from the influence of
which I cannot recover. I thought I was in a large
forest abroad, and as I travelled through it I saw
coming towards me, but still at a considerable distance
from me, a solitary horseman. In spite of the space
between us, his face and mien were distinctly visible
to me, every feature being clearly apparent. As I
watched him advance, three men sprang out of a
thicket, and, seizing his horse by the bridle roughly
pulled him from it and proceeded to search him.
Then I woke, but shortly again fell asleep, when,
although the surroundings were different, my former
vision was resumed. It was still a foreign country.
The spot was, I somehow knew, not far from a large
town. A great concourse of people seemed to be
assembled, and surrounded a gibbet, and, as I gazed,
I saw the figure of my previous dream, attired in the

uniform of a British officer, being prepared for execution. Then I saw him strung up and hanged.
This has made so strong an impression on me that I
cannot shake it off.'

Almost as he spoke, the door opened, and Miss
Seward, accompanied by André, entered, when, to
Mr Cunningham's wonderment and consternation, he
beheld in his guest the prototype of his dream.

André was now under sailing orders for America.
He landed at Philadelphia in the autumn of 1774, and
gave himself up to the study of his profession, winning golden opinions for ability and energy. He was
at this time slight in figure, and of martial and upright
bearing; his countenance was intelligent in expression and his features noble in cast, while his complexion and smile were youthful and bright. To a
keen and vigorous understanding was added a charm
of manner and a winning courtesy of demeanour
that never failed to attract all those with whom he
was brought in contact. In deeds of daring he was
ever foremost, and when the time came that the endurance and stability of his nature were put to a
crucial test, his dauntless courage and chivalrous action won the respect and admiration of the whole
civilised world. The gallant heart that met death in
one of its most formidable aspects and shrank not,
that was content to suffer, provided that those who
loved him and whom he loved should experience no
pang of self-reproach, was apparent in many of the
war-scenes in which he took part. Time went on,

and night surprises at Paoli and elsewhere, the reduction of Verplank, together with many a brush with
the enemy, had familiarised him with the horrors of
the battle-field, but these never seemed to blunt the
keenness of his sensitiveness or do aught but quicken
his desire to relieve and lighten the sufferings and
sorrows of friends and foes. He was with the troops
that were sent down to garrison St John's, after
Ticonderoga had fallen into the enemy's hands, and
was there taken prisoner. The captives were treated
with great harshness by the Americans, and despoiled
of all their private effects, and that André's passion
for Honora was not extinct is shown in a sentence
contained in one of his letters to a friend :—' They took
from me all I had,' he says, ' except Honora's mini-
ature which I concealed in my mouth, and, though
preserving nothing else, yet deemed myself rich.' He
was, after thirteen months' captivity, exchanged, and
he returned to his duties, leaving behind him an exceptional reputation for courage, endurance, and kindness, and having transformed many a foe into a friend.
The society in which he had spent the days of his
early manhood had developed his taste for literature
and art. He drew and painted well, and the letters
which have been preserved from his pen, although
couched in the somewhat stilted style of the period,
yet record such delicacy of feeling and ease of diction
that they stamp him at once as a cultivated and proficient writer. Soon after his release he was promoted to a captaincy, and became aide-de-camp to

Sir Charles Grey, a General of Division. His lively descriptions of his adventures, illustrated with much skill, humour and artistic merit, together with his graphic and intelligent accounts of the circumstances of his captivity, gained for him much notice from the commander-in-chief, who was quick to recognise his talents.

We must now direct our attention to the pivot upon which André's tragic history turns. In proportion as his fate appeals to our sympathies and his character to our admiration, so great are the repugnance and indignation with which we regard Benedict Arnold— a traitor, than whom no blacker specimen disfigures the pages of history. In spite, however, of the gigantic treason which he attempted and with which his name must ever be associated in the annals of the American War of Independence, he was one of those anomalies that seem to be formed to puzzle the student of human nature, possessing two entirely different sides to his character. A man of power, talent and energy, often generous, always enterprising and adventurous — the story of the attempted betrayal of his country and comrades cannot but fill any generous mind with abhorrence and indignation. From his earliest youth, he had been impatient of all control, and filled with a conviction of his own superior merits. He brooked neither rivalry from his equals, nor interference from his superiors. Love of praise and love of money, 'those two corrupters of mankind,' stifled his compensating qualities, and when the first failed

he flew to the second, and covered himself with ignominy and disgrace. Between 1765 and 1770 he
was actively engaged in business in Newhaven. He
was made captain of the governour's guard there,
a militia regiment, composed of young men of the
city. In 1775 the first collision between the British
and the American troops took place, resulting in the
defeat of the former. On receipt of this news, Arnold
called together his Newhaven company, and after
rousing their enthusiasm by an eloquent appeal to
their patriotism and after defying the civil authorities,
who demurred at supplying him with the materials
for war that he not only claimed as a right, but threatened to possess himself of by force—a demand, however that they ultimately yielded—he marched his men
to Cambridge in Massachusetts, the head-quarters of
the troops who had collected there to resist the further incursions of the British.

Here he waited on their 'Committee of Safety,' and
propounded the scheme of the surprise of Ticonderoga,
obtained from them a colonel's command in their
state's service, and started on his way, enlisting men
on the road, having been granted supplies for the purpose. Within twenty-two miles of their destination,
they overtook a body of men who called themselves
the 'Green Mountain Boys,' who came from Connecticut and who had started on the same enterprise.
Arnold at once claimed the command of the whole,
which claim was of course resisted, but seeing that
he could not prevail, he wisely yielded, and joining

issue, the two bodies of men assaulted Ticonderoga, and Arnold and the commander entered the fort side by side as it fell before the unexpected onslaught. After this had been acomplished, Arnold, with persistent arrogance, again endeavoured to oust Allan violently from the command, but the latter was chosen by the troops, and so he was obliged to give way. His presumptuous action was reported to the Massachusetts committee, who, feeling responsible for his conduct, sent three of their members to Lake Champlain, where he had taken up his abode. He had gone thither, possessed himself of a schooner seized from a British agent, armed it, sailed down to St John's, a port situated on the lake, surprised the garrison, taken possession of a king's sloop and four batteaux, together with a quantity of valuable stores, and returned triumphantly to Ticonderoga. He now considered himself the commander of the navy, and finally selecting another port on Lake Champlain as his quarters resolved to defy the enemy who, it was rumoured, would shortly arrive in force. He had thus obtained a temporary control of an important portion of the highway between New York and Canada, to say nothing of the stores so much needed by the colonists.

Meantime, however, his previous conduct was being investigated by the Massachusetts delegates, and they proceeded to Crown Point where he had taken up his quarters, to lay their instructions before him. Arnold's arrogance and indignation were irrepressible; he bitterly complained of the insult thus put upon

him, and throwing up his command refused to be
subjected to such indignities. His accounts in connection with the land expedition were examined, and
although grave doubts were entertained with regard
to their accuracy, they were settled, and thus ended
his first adventure, and thus began his standing and
. ever-growing grievance against his country. It is
easy to read between the lines and see how much
there was to be desired, as in a young and inex-
perienced country there could not fail to be, in the
way of discipline and organisation in the scattered
American camp, but the appointment of Washington
about this time, to the command of the whole continental army, partook of the nature of an inspiration,
without which the cause of the colonists would almost
certainly have been, at all events temporarily, lost.
When he assumed the command in 1775, he had
already resolved to attempt the military possession
of Canada, which colony was showing every sign of
loyalty to Great Britain. Washington's lieutenant,
General Montgomery, advanced by Lakes Champlain
and George, and entering Canada, wrested Montreal
from the English and waited for the carrying out of
the rest of Washington's daring plan. This was a
proposition that a body of men should traverse the
wilderness that lay beyond the mountains of Maine,
between Canada and New York, by the Kennebec
River, to Quebec, and there co-operate with Montgomery. The proposed expedition was one fraught
with dangers and difficulties, and required a leader

bold, skilful, and enterprising. Arnold was chosen
by Washington for the execution of this hazardous
undertaking, and the result proved that these qualities
had not been by any means unduly ascribed to him.
The country, wild, untrodden, unexplored by civilised
man, was a network of lakes, rivers, falls and natural
obstacles of all kinds, the men had to be provided
with canoes, which they carried on their shoulders, to
cross the rivers. It is impossible in such a paper to
give a detailed account of the hardships they endured,
but it is certain that Arnold possessed the invaluable
quality of inspiring confidence in his followers. Their
sufferings—it was during the winter months—and
their bravery and endurance have probably not often
been exceeded in the annals of war, but it must suffice
here to say that, after almost superhuman efforts,
after the desertion and retreat of a portion of the little
army, under the influence and orders of the second
in command, after a reduction of the valiant force
from its original number of 1100, to 675, they burst
through the forest encircling Quebec, and arrived
opposite that city, half-starved and exhausted, after
two months of terrible privations and trials, borne
with the utmost heroism and fortitude. Montgomery
joined Arnold, and on the 31st December 1775, the
two commanders led the assault on the city of Quebec.
It proved however, not only unsuccessful, but disastrous, for Montgomery was killed and Arnold badly
shot in the leg. He was not long in recovering sufficiently to be able to give instructions from his couch,

K

and thus the siege of Quebec was kept up, to Washington's great approval and satisfaction, and Arnold was triumphantly promoted to the rank of Brigadier-General by Congress.

He retired to Montreal, suffering severely from his wound, and here he was at the head of affairs. During his stay he seized goods for the service belonging to merchants of the city, and much quarrelling and recrimination followed. Disputes between himself and his brother officers were also rife, for he was constantly insubordinate to his superiors, and insolent and overbearing to both equals and superiors. Large sums were claimed by the despoiled merchants, and a court-martial on the second in command ensued—Arnold casting back the blame upon him. During its progress, he wrote an insulting letter to the officers who composed it, who demanded an apology, which Arnold promptly and insolently refused. These matters were reported to General Gates, who had been appointed before to the command of the army in Canada, and who made the grave error of condoning his offences for the sake of retaining his services. Thus, brilliant actions and grave and weighty charges against him, continually oscillated in his career, but it cannot be denied that he commanded as he fought, with consummate ability and courage. On quitting Canada, he established himself, with Gates' approval, once more on Lake Champlain, and secured the command of a little squadron of fighting vessels which had been placed there, to oppose the advance of the

British, whose object was to obtain naval suprem-
acy there, and effect a junction ultimately with the
king's troops at New York. The British flotilla was
largely in excess of Arnold's, but undaunted by their
vast superiority of numbers, he fiercely attacked them
on the 11th October 1776, and after a desperate
struggle of many hours' duration, when night fell,
availed himself of the darkness and of a friendly fog,
and escaped through the very midst of the enemy's
fleet. Some of his ships were captured and some
escaped, and after fighting for four more hours, he ran
the remaining vessels ashore, set them on fire, their
flags still flying, and escaped with their crews to
Ticonderoga through the forest.

After this brilliant exploit he joined Gates' army.
Washington's approval was cordially expressed, but
the still undecided matter of the goods seized at
Montreal influenced both the opinions and the
actions of Congress, who emphasised their doubts
in February 1777 by appointing five new major-
generals in the army and passing over Arnold who
was senior to them all. Washington was nearly as
concerned as himself, and took active steps to have
the slight removed, but to no purpose. Five months
later, when on his way to Philadelphia with a few
hundred militia, Arnold had a brush with some
British troops and dispersed them, and in acknow-
ledgment of this service he was raised to the rank of
major-general and was at the same time presented
by Congress with a horse, 'properly caparisoned.'

It would be as unnecessary as impossible to follow Arnold through all his campaigns ; it will suffice to say that he quarrelled with Gates, who appears to have regarded him with doubt not unmingled with suspicion. He was confined within camp, by Gates' orders, during the battle of Saratoga, on the 17th October 1777. For some time he endured the indignity, but at last his resentment and impatience became intolerable, and he galloped on to the field. This act of insubordination coming to Gates' knowledge, he sent orders to him instantly to return to camp. The messenger rode full gallop after him, but was out-distanced, and Arnold, seeking the hottest part of the fight, issued orders everywhere, distinguishing himself for his gallantry and coolness ; indeed, it is asserted by some that it was owing to his exertions and ability that the British were routed. He stormed the lines leading the van, and was shot in the same leg that received the wound before Quebec. He was removed to Albany, where he remained invalided during the winter. Meantime, Philadelphia had been invested by the English in 1777, but their occupation did not prove of much service to their arms, and in 1778 the British Government recalled Sir William Howe, at that officer's own request, and replaced him by Sir Henry Clinton, who arrived in June, bringing with him orders for the evacuation of the town. During the winter, the officers had greatly ingratiated themselves with the inhabitants, who were warmly in favour of British rule. A grand *fête*, called the

'Mischianza,' only mentioned here in consequence of
the wide-spread notoriety that, for some insufficient
reason it obtained at the time, was given in honour of
the departing commander-in-chief, and on the 18th
of June the army quitted the town. Washington had
been encamped all the winter at Valley Forge—a
village some few miles distant from Philadelphia—
keenly watching the movements of the enemy. His
army—ragged, hungry, barefoot—had neither coats
nor shirts, shoes nor stockings, their sole attempt at
uniformity being the sticking in their hats—or rather
in the hats of those that were fortunate enough to
possess such an appendage—small boughs of trees.
They were often for days without proper food, men
and horses on the brink of starvation. Thus the
movement of the British troops must have been
indeed a welcome incident to the American general,
who directed Arnold who was still suffering from his
wound and unable for much active service, but who
had joined the army at Valley Forge, to take military
command at Philadelphia, giving him at the same
time the most stringent instructions to do all in his
power to propitiate the inhabitants.

Arnold entered the town on the 19th June. The
temptation involved in the possession of such unlimited power, as the command of a city by martial law, proved, as was to be expected, too much for
his powers of self-repression, and he promptly entered
into certain contracts with the clothier-general of the
army and another, that they should jointly benefit by

certain transactions. Rumour soon spread the fact
among the citizens that Arnold was personally interested in the government purchases, and although
the whole truth was not divulged till after his name
had become infamous by his treason, the character that
he had acquired by similar practices at Montreal had
preceded him to Philadelphia, and he was regarded
with suspicion and dislike. He took up his abode in
the house that had been occupied by Sir William
Howe, and entered on a style of living far beyond his
means. By degrees, and as civil authority was restored, his absolute power became more limited, but
his arbitrary and arrogant conduct rendered him
supremely unpopular, and he was more than once
attacked by an angry mob. Not only did his money
affairs, which he vainly strove to redeem by speculations which plunged him deeper and deeper into difficulties, press heavily upon him, but he engaged in an
angry controversy with the Council of Philadelphia
who administered a severe public rebuke, resolving
that he was unworthy of his rank and station, and dis-
respectful to the supreme authority of the state. His
offences were enumerated and included a wilful abuse
of power, and an unjustifiable interference with the
rights of the people. The most serious charge—that
of speculating with public money—was not then sustained for want of evidence, but it was ultimately
proved. A court-martial was convened by Congress
to investigate the matter, and Arnold resolved to
advocate his own cause. Bronzed, crippled, defiant

and arrogant, he came into the court, and founded his defence on his services to his country, while his speech contained something more than an insinuation of treason and meditated desertion on the part of certain of his comrades, a design which it will be seen later, had already been for several months under his own consideration. He read aloud Washington's complimentary letters to himself, including one which had accompanied a present of epaulettes and sword knots, and with haughty and bombastic self-satisfaction, pointed to his wounds, his merits, and his sacrifices. His representations however did not satisfy the tribunal, and although he was acquitted of some of the charges, he was found guilty of others, and the court sentenced him to be reprimanded by the commander-in-chief, who, during the whole of Arnold's chequered career, had evinced the utmost tenderness towards his failings, and whose leniency is not, in our opinion, accounted for satisfactorily, even by the latter's unquestionable valour and ability. Washington performed the unpleasant duty assigned to him with a clemency and forbearance worthy of a better cause, couching the obligatory reproof in such noble and dignified language that it conveyed at least as much praise as censure :—

'Our profession,' he said, 'is the chastest of all ; the shadow of a fault tarnishes our most brilliant actions. The least inadvertence may cause us to lose that public favour which it is so hard to gain. I reprimand you for having forgotten that, in proportion as

you have rendered yourself formidable to our enemies,
you should have shown moderation to our citizens.
Exhibit again those splendid qualities which have
placed you in the rank of our most distinguished
generals. As far as it shall be in my power, I myself
will furnish you with opportunities for regaining the
esteem which you formerly enjoyed.'

Unmoved by his commander's generosity, and very
likely incapable of realising the subtle and chivalrous
appeal contained in his words, it was now that Arnold,
clothed in the armour of his so-called wrongs, finally
discarded his country's cause and resolved to wreak
his vengeance on her. He had already presented to
Congress large claims against the United States on
account of moneys paid by him when serving them at
different times, and now he renewed his petition for
their settlement. By these means he hoped to extricate himself from his liabilities, but the commissioners
appointed to investigate these claims, reduced them
very considerably, and although he appealed against
their decision, Congress endorsed their verdict, adding,
at the same time, that, in their opinion, more had been
allowed him than he was entitled to. Before the
court-martial had finished their sittings, Arnold had
thrown up his command, and it was during these tem-
pestuous months—for, in consequence of the constant
changes of officers and of other circumstances inseparable from a country in a state of war, the trial
had been a long time pending—that he married Miss
Shippen, the daughter of a gentleman of high standing

in Philadelphia, who, during the occupation of the British, had been much admired and sought after by the society that surrounded the English commander-in-chief.

The Shippens' sympathies were entirely with the old country, and a friendship had sprung up between Miss Shippen and André, and after the evacuation of the town a correspondence had been carried on between them. André's heart was still true to Honora, and it is to be understood that their affection for one another was friendship in the strictest sense of the term. Arnold, perceiving that in this state of things lay his possible opportunity, encouraged the friendship and the correspondence with his wife, and it was doubtless through this medium that he made his first cautious advances to Clinton. It is here to be noted that André had joined Clinton's staff when General Grey had quitted his command and gone to England.

The specific treason however, that Arnold proposed to carry out later, could at this earlier period, hardly have suggested itself to him, as he could not have foreseen the way in which matters would adjust themselves, but we suppose that he saw the probability at no very distant date, of creating for himself some possible means whereby he might betray some strategical scheme to the enemy, and thus win for himself a large pecuniary reward and at the same time bring destruction on the hopes of those who had dealt him such bitter humiliations. Meantime, he had purchased a country-seat close to Philadelphia where he re-

sided with his wife in a recklessly extravagant manner.
He entertained lavishly, kept a large stud of horses,
and remained at Mount Pleasant until he was appointed to the command of West Point—and here his
eldest son was born.

Early in the spring of 1778, a draft of what was then
called 'The Conciliatory Bills,' had been sent to
America by the British Government, to attempt a negotiation to effect a compromise and a reconciliation between the two countries. But independence had been
purchased far too dearly to be so easily resigned,—
it was the outcome of too much bloodshed, of too
many sacrifices, to be relinquished for a few soft words
and vague promises, and the Americans determined
that their hardly-won triumph should be maintained
if necessary at the point of the bayonet, and the unsuccessful commissioners returned whence they came, foiled
and frustrated in their endeavours. The Americans
were now indeed giving the English cause to rue the
day when the mother-country had pushed them to
the extremity that had transformed them from loyal
and faithful subjects into an injured and indignant
people,—a people urged by a sense of self-respect,
justice and dignity to have recourse to arms to rid
themselves of a yoke that had become intolerable.
About this time an event occurred which filled them
with hope and joy. The King of France, who had
for some time supplied them with arms and war
material, and, moreover, had increased his own arma-
ments with scarcely concealed hostility to England,

suddenly and openly negotiated a treaty of peace and commerce with America, formally recognising her independence, and signing conventions of defensive alliance, including an undertaking not to lay down his own arms, until his ally's independence were acknowledged by the English. This action on the part of France was, of course, considered by all as equivalent to a declaration of war against England, and the British ambassador at Paris was recalled. Clinton's exit from Philadelphia (1778) had been hastened by the rumour of the departure from the shores of France of a large squadron of ships of war, bound, as it was believed for the Delaware, on which river that city is situated. He shipped many of his troops thence to New York—as many as he could find transport for— but he was compelled to lead the greater portion across the state of New Jersey, which divides Philadelphia from the sea, to embark them at Sandy Hook for New York. As soon as Washington—encamped as we have said at Valley Forge—heard of the movement of the enemy, he launched a portion of his army, under Lafayette, who had fought under Washington and had been made a major-general in the American service the year before, to follow, and harass them. An encounter ensued, which was curtailed by the fall of evening, and when morning broke it was discovered that in the darkness of night, Clinton had silently withdrawn his men. Lafayette did not pursue, so Clinton made the best of his way across New Jersey to Sandy Hook, where Lord Howe's fleet was in readi-

ness to embark them for New York. On the 22d July
the expected French ships arrived, but the hoped-for
encounter between the British and French fleets was
avoided by the French admiral who sailed at once to
Rhode Island, leaving Lord Howe unmolested in the
bay of New York—and Washington went into quarters
on the west side of the Hudson, a few miles above
West Point.

The river Hudson cuts three hundred miles of the
great continent of America in two, running due north
and south, and flowing into the Atlantic at New York,
of which town, as has been seen, the British were in
possession. Free comunication between that city and
Canada, by the river and through Lakes Champlain
and George at its northermost point, was a project the
success of which was of vital importance to the British
arms, in order to consolidate the allegiance of the
colony and bring them in touch with their own people,
whilst the failure of this scheme was, of course, of
equally radical moment to the Americans. The Hudson
is navigable for ships of sixty guns, and in order to
obstruct any British naval forces that should adventure
its ascent, a point of land twenty-five miles north of
New York, jutting out into the river on its west side,
surmounted by high rocks and hills, had been fortified by the Americans with every appliance of the
engineer's art. A range of fortifications had been
formed from the bottom to the highest mount, on the
top of which a fort had been erected, unassailable from
its commanding position, stocked with every species

of military store, and supplied with all means of defence and defiance, it was at once the arsenal of the continental army and the supreme bulwark of its desperate resistance.

Months wore on, and 1780 found Benedict Arnold watching in eager suspense and vigilant anxiety, the movements and counter-movements of the opposing forces. Greed for money was his ruling passion, which, fostered by revenge, overpowered every other desire of his being, and it was just before the evacuation of Philadelphia by the English that he launched his first anonymous communication to Clinton, conveying sundry hints of conditional betrayal of secrets of importance. At first Sir Henry received these offers coldly, but he did not entirely ignore them, believing that he might possibly glean some important information from his correspondent. Other letters from the same hand followed him to New York, and it became gradually manifest that the writer possessed much knowledge of military matters as well of circumstances and contingencies, that could only be known to one moving in the highest military circles. In 1780, when the command of West Point was pending, the correspondence was reopened, the writer stating that he expected to be immediately given a most important command, and concluding his letter by the direct offer of surrendering, by some means afterwards to be decided upon, the whole of the West Point military position. By this act, Benedict proved how confident he was of his unlimited influence over

Washington, for as yet no advances had been made
by Arnold with respect to the appointment. This
convincing proof of the rank of his correspondent
caused the English commander's heart to beat high
with hopeful anticipation. By one *coup-de-main* to gain
possession of West Point—the Gibraltar of America,
the key to the position, to make its garrison prisoners,
to acquire all their stores and provisions, to obtain the
command of the coveted highway to Canada—would
be a triumph, a success, that Clinton could not have
anticipated in his wildest dreams. American independence, that had been (as Great Britain averred so
presumptuously, and as America deemed so right-
eously) taken possession of, would be crushed and
destroyed, and in all human probability the war would
terminate with a brilliant and triumphant victory for
our arms.

The standard of rectitude, virtue and honour, under-
goes such depreciation when under the influence of
the two extremes of human passion and emergency,
that it would be futile to dream of measuring men's
actions by that which serves them as a rule on less
momentous occasions. That all is fair in love and
war is an adage artfully and skilfully, if somewhat
licentiously, adapted to the weakness of human nature.
It has been accepted from time immemorial as an
excuse for the lowering of that standard,—it obtains
under the pressure of certain overwhelming eventu-
alities, and it has been accepted and practically
acquiesced in by all. Thus the participation or con-

nivance in an otherwise dishonourable design—in a
stratagem unworthy in any other phase of perplexity
or danger—is regarded by the spectators with toleration, and by those immediately concerned, with
approval and applause. André's actions, the account
of which follows, were in strict accordance with his
general's instructions, which again were modelled
upon the elastic principles of civilised warfare. Moreover, the Americans, as viewed by Great Britain, and
from a perfectly reasonable and fair standpoint, were
insurgents and rebels, and indeed sympathise as we
may with their hard position and intolerable provo-
cation, they were. Shortly before these events Clinton,
who entertained the highest opinion of his young
aide-de-camp's capacities and character, but whose
military status was only that of a captain, wrote to
the authorities at home, requesting that he should
be raised to the rank of major, his object being to
confer upon him the appointment of deputy adjutant-
general, a post untenable by anyone of inferior degree.
The application was couched in terms of the highest
eulogy, and described him as 'an invaluable young
man, adorned with the rarest endowments of education
and nature, who could not but attain to the highest
honours of his profession.' The petition was refused,
but on Clinton expressing his extreme displeasure at
the indifference shown to his requests, the decision
was reconsidered, and the request granted, the official
appointment arriving at New York two days after
André's death. Meantime, he had been performing

the duties of deputy adjutant - general for some
months.

Just at this time the English fleet was augmented,
and in spite of the belief entertained by the Americans
that that of France was its superior, it was deemed
unwise to put their opinion to the proof. So Washington paused in his operations, proposing to wait
until such time as Admiral de Ternay should be reinforced. Clinton now made preparations for a combined attack by land and sea on the French at Newport,
but this time the American forces were increased, so
he landed his men on Long Island, and himself returned to New York.

Thus, in manœuvring and counter-manœuvring, the
season wore on, and on 31st July, Arnold, probably
for the purpose of contriving the interview that
followed, came from Mount Pleasant, on feigned
business, to Connecticut. He rode up and joined the
American commander-in-chief as the latter was
superintending the crossing of the last division of his
army to the eastern side of the Hudson, and was
heartily welcomed by him. Washington conversed
eagerly with him on the prospects of the war, and
communicated with him his project of marching his
army to New York across the White Plains which lie
to the north-east of the city, in order to attack it in
its weakened state, many of Clinton's men being on
Long Island. Arnold cautiously opened up the business that he had really come from Philadelphia to
inquire about. ' Has any post been assigned to me ? '

he asked. 'I offer you,' answered Washington, 'the command of the left wing of the attacking forces—it is the post of honour.' He then invited him to ride up to head-quarters with him, and on his way thither learned, to his great surprise, that his magnificent offer was refused. Arnold complained of his wound, although there were at this time few signs of its incapacitating him; he declared that he was not fit for active service, and he concluded by preferring the request that the command of West Point should be conferred upon him. Washington did not conceal his astonishment; he had been casting about for a general of adequate abilities to command his left on the proposed important expedition, and both his thoughts and his wishes had flown to Arnold. The command was one for which he considered Arnold's attributes eminently qualified him; it was obvious there was no serious physical obstruction, while the appointment offered every attraction for a brave, capable and ambitious general, and was at the same time an honour that implied not only pardon for past offences, but confidence in future achievements, whereas the post at West Point would require no skill, and could be productive of no glory. It has been said that there are occasions in everyone's life when his actions are in direct opposition to the bent of his character, and it appears to us that Washington's whole policy, as regards his dealings with Arnold, is an illustration of the truth of this assertion. That he should have recognised in him a capable general, whose abilities

L 4

were splendid, whose courage was unassailable, and whose endurance was proverbial, is natural enough, but that a man of Washington's upright, almost stern, rectitude of character, should have condoned offences of such a nature as had been committed by Arnold, and of which he had been actually found guilty, is, in our opinion, quite incomprehensible. Time after time had he fallen under the ban of Congress for conduct unbecoming an officer and a gentleman, and yet Washington regarded his faults with tenderness, and ignoring the unquestionable justice of the blame accorded to him, strove to reinstate him in the public service. His wound was healed and he seemed in robust health, but in spite of these glaring and incontrovertible facts, he declined, on the plea of ill-health, the means so generously offered him of clearing his besmirched character and of winning renown.

With some reluctance then, Washington granted his request, and nominated him to the coveted command, and the first days of August 1780 saw Arnold established at Beverley, the country seat of a Colonel Beverley Robinson, whose property, in consequence of his loyalty to the British cause, had been confiscated by the State of New York. It was a picturesque mansion, situated on the eastern side of the river, just opposite to West Point, high up from the stream, but at the foot of a mountain covered with woods. Here he was joined by his wife and child early in the month of September. He seems to have secluded himself as much as possible from the society of his officers, and is described at this time as being stern, preoccupied and gloomy.

Fully to comprehend what follows, a slight description of the river Hudson, between New York and West Point, on both banks, is necessary. West Point is situated twenty-five miles north of New York, on the western side, and between the two places, and also on the western side the following ferries and villages occur, starting from the north :—Stony Point, King's Ferry, Haverstraw Bay and village, Tappan, and Dobbs' Ferry. On the eastern side and in the same order, are Verplank's Ferry, Teller's Point, Tarrytown and Dobbs' Ferry, the corresponding landing-place to the one on the western side of that name. The White Plains extend to the east and south of Tarrytown, and lie between the latter and north-west New York, while Dobbs' Ferry is two miles south of Tappan. Except at King's Ferry, Teller's Point and Dobbs' Ferry, the river is five miles broad, but at the places named it narrows and it is considerably narrower between King's Ferry and West Point. It had now become indispensable for the success of the plot that an interview to adjust the necessary preparations must take place. The correspondence was being carried on between Arnold and André, on behalf of Sir Henry Clinton, under feigned names, and in metaphorical language, Arnold assuming the *nom de guerre* of Gustavus, and André that of John Anderson.

It offered few difficulties, being under the direction of one in whom so much power was centred as in

Arnold. Many plans were suggested by both parties
before one satisfactory to bcth was decided upon, and
Arnold made it very clear that he would take no self-
compromising step till such time as Clinton would
bind himself to a definite, and what he himself considered sufficient reward. The money to be gained by the
transaction was a matter that he very resolutely decided should not be left to chance, or to Clinton's
generosity after its completion. Although he had
hitherto had no confidant on his own side, Arnold
had written to Beverley Robinson, saying that, in
consequence of the treatment he had received from
his country, he had changed his principles, and he
now sought to restore himself to his king's favour by
a signal service that he was about to reveal to Clinton.

The plot was this:—On a specified day, Clinton,
with Arnold's connivance, was to enter West Point
with his army; Arnold, who was to affect surprise,
was to despatch a messenger to Washington, conveying such false or garbled intelligence as would ensure
his hastening thither in person with his troops, and
the British soldiers would then surprise and take him
and his advancing battalions prisoners, the approaches
to the stronghold being well adapted to the success of
such a scheme—to all these arrangements it is stated
Beverley Robinson was privy. Both correspondents
now couched their letters in terms intelligible only to
each other, which seemed to allude to Robinson's
house, which had been confiscated by the Americans,
and which was the supposed subject of the bargaining.

Arnold endeavoured to persuade Clinton to send
André within the American lines for the purpose of
the interview, but this suggestion was at once rejected
by Clinton, and Dobbs' Ferry, though with an unaccountable indefiniteness as regarded which side of the
river, was then decided upon, and on the 10th September Arnold left his head-quarters at Robinson's
house and went five miles down the river to King's
Ferry in his barge, passing the night at the house of one
Joshua Smith, near Haverstraw Bay, five miles further
on, and of whom more hereafter. But as the next
morning Arnold's barge approached Dobbs' Ferry,
a distance of about ten miles from where he had
spent the night, some British gun-boats fired upon
him and he was compelled to beat a hasty retreat,
only just escaping capture. Thus the proposed meeting failed. Arnold was, of course, well known, so it
was necessary to account to Washington, who would
be likely to hear of his appearance there, for his
presence so far south. This he did by writing to the
commander-in-chief, stating that he had come down
the river to see to the establishing of some signals.
A little after sunset he returned to Robinson's house,
this was on the 11th September.

Thus baulked, it became necessary to arrange
another meeting. Again Dobbs' Ferry was fixed
as the trysting place, and Arnold arranged to meet
André there on the night of September 20th. 'It
will be necessary for you to be in disguise,' he wrote.
'I can't be more explicit now, but meet me if pos-

sible, and rest assured that if there is no danger in passing your lines, you will be safe where I propose a meeting.' Anxious to bring so momentous a scheme to a conclusion, Clinton, before the above letter had arrived at its destination, had already sent Beverley Robinson as far up the river as circumstances would admit in the war-ship *Vulture*, in order, if possible, to reopen communications with Arnold. He retained André however with him at New York, in case of the arrival of any letter from the former, a contingency that came to pass. The *Vulture* dropped anchor at Teller's Point—midway between Dobbs' Ferry and King's Ferry, and a letter was despatched, under the protection of a flag, to the officers in command at Verplank's Ferry, with a request that it might be forwarded to Arnold at Robinson's house. It so happened that Washington had arranged to meet the general in command of the French forces—Rochambeau—at Hartford in Connecticut, and that it was his intention to cross the Hudson at King's Ferry with some of his staff on this very day. The letter from the *Vulture*, had been duly despatched immediately on its arrival at Verplank to Arnold at Robinson's house by the officer in command, and had reached the general just before he left his quarters for the purpose of officially receiving the commander-in-chief with due respect and honour. At the time of its delivery Arnold was in the company of some of his staff, and he mentioned to them the (ostensible) purport of the despatch, viz., the negotiation concerning Robinson's property. One of the officers expressed his surprise that any such correspondence should have been opened, saying that the civil authorities could alone adjudicate in such a case.

Proceeding down the river however, Arnold received Washington at Stoney Point, and they crossed together to Verplank's Ferry in Arnold's barge. The *Vulture* lay about five miles off, below Teller's Point, and was of course the subject of much remark and conjecture. Pursuing his crafty tactics, Arnold showed the letter he had received to Washington, and asked for instructions concerning it. The commander-in-chief at once expressed disapproval of the correspondence, also asserting that it was a subject for the civil courts, adding that such communications gave grounds for suspicion, and discountenanced the interview suggested by the writer. Having landed the general at Verplank, Arnold returned to his quarters to make final arrangements for the prosecution of his perfidious design. Able, in consequence of his last manœuvre, to act in apparent harmony with Washington's instructions, he openly sent a flag boat to the *Vulture,* conveying not the gist of his general's orders but the intelligence, in disguised language that on the night of the 20th he would probably come himself or else send someone on board who should be furnished with a flag of truce, and in whom absolute confidence could be placed. ' I expect General Washington on Saturday,' he added, 'and will lay before him what you wish to communi-

cate,' thus conveying the intelligence of Washington's
movements, and giving the appearance, in case of
detection, of writing on public business. Robinson at
once dispatched this communication to Clinton at
New York, who received it the same night, and next
morning André quitted New York and arrived on
board the *Vulture* at seven p.m.

He had received definite and specific orders from
Sir Henry. He was not to enter the enemy's lines,
he was on no account to carry any papers on his
person, and he was forbidden to wear any other dress
than his uniform, although Arnold had especially en-
joined that he should be in disguise. Arnold's plan,
however, was laid with a more definite view to his own
safety than to that of André, and this was a fact that
must have been patent to Clinton and which of course
the latter did all in his power to neutralise. To be
compelled to trust to such an one as Arnold was an
element of danger from which there was no escape,
and from which the other side was free. Arnold
always intended that the interview should take place
on the western side of the river, and near to—if possible within—the American lines, in spite of Clinton.
The general, Arnold's predecessor in the command at
West Point, had been in the habit of employing one
Joshua Smith, who lived in a small house a short distance from Haverstraw, to collect intelligence of the
enemy from New York. Smith held a good position
in society, and Arnold kept his eye upon him as a
desirable instrument for his ends. Smith was always

furnished with a written permission to pass the
American lines, and Arnold decided that, should
occasion arise, his house should be used as a place of
concealment. When Arnold had visited him before
on the 10th, he had prevailed upon him to be a party
to, and an actor in, the drama that followed, although
it is still an open question as to whether he was a
dupe or an accomplice. At anyrate, Arnold's intention was to send Smith to the *Vulture* in order to
bring André ashore, and that the meeting, upon which
hung such momentous possibilities, should take place
in the immediate neighbourhood of his house. All
this was accomplished, though with a considerable
amount of difficulty. A boat was obtained, which
was despatched to a creek in Haverstraw Bay two
miles below Smith's house, a countersign was agreed
upon, and the commanders of American gun-boats
informed that they were employed in obtaining intelligence of the enemy, and the boatmen were induced,
in spite of great reluctance on their part, and finally
in response to many threats and promises of reward
on Arnold's, to row out to the *Vulture*, and at eleven
p.m., Smith, accompanied by the two boatmen, pushed
off from Haverstraw Creek bound on an expedition,
the perils of which were not realised by any of the
three.

The night was calm and still, the oars had been
muffled, and the boat glided swiftly and silently
through the water, reaching its destination without
interruption or accident of any kind. No one on

board, save André, Robinson and the captain, Sutherland by name, was aware of the matter in hand, and a torrent of oaths and abuse from the officers on watch greeted the adventurers as they passed under the ship's bows. They were ordered alongside, and under the cover of the darkness, Smith clambered up the side of the *Vulture*. Much doubt and consternation were evinced by André and Robinson at the arrival of Smith. They had expected Arnold in person, and his substitute was an unknown actor, one of whom they knew nothing, and whom they were thus compelled to take on trust. Robinson strongly objected to the risk of sending André under circumstances so changed in complexion, but André's eagerness to accomplish an enterprise that had already failed once, caused him to persist, and in a few minutes he had taken his place in the boat. He was clothed, according to his general's orders, in his uniform, which was, however, entirely covered with a large blue great-coat. Smith either believed or pretended to believe that he was a private friend of Robinson, and was either really ignorant of his name, occupation and character, or simulated ignorance. He had, moreover, expected Robinson to go ashore with them. They left the ship and landed at the appointed spot, six miles below Stoney Point. Hither Arnold had arrived on horseback, accompanied by one of Smith's servants on another horse, and as the boat grated on the shingle, André lept out and ran up the bank, followed by Smith. Here they found Arnold con-

cealed amongst the thick bushes and trees. Leaving
André and Arnold together, Smith, at the request of
the latter, returned to the boat where the men, fatigued
by their efforts, soon fell asleep. Not so Smith.
Offended and mortified by his exclusion from the
conference, he remained there only as long as his
patience endured, and the interview proving long, he
presently crept up the bank and warned the conspira-
tors, that morning would soon dawn, and that the
boat must be moved from its present position to
escape detection. Clearly however, a satisfactory conclusion had not yet been arrived at, for, consenting
that the boat should be removed, Arnold remounted
his horse, André got on the servant's, and they
wended their way to Smith's house, two or three
miles along the road northwards.

Passing through Haverstraw village, the sentry's
challenge announced that they were entering the
enemy's lines, and the peril of the position became
apparent to André. The situation was unexpected
—impossible to retreat—unwillingly acting in direct
opposition to his general's orders—there was yet no
alternative but to advance under Arnold's guidance
and to meet the emergency as best he could. He
would have returned to the *Vulture*, but the preliminaries had not been settled. He must have known the
character of the man in whose hands he had placed
himself, and probably felt very doubtful as to the
issue. Just as they arrived at Smith's house, a loud
cannonade boomed from the river. The officer at

Teller's Point had begun to bombard the *Vulture* in order to force her to remove from what he deemed too close a proximity to land. This had the desired effect. The *Vulture* dropped several miles down the river, and further from Smith's house. The consultation between the contracting parties was resumed, and at length the conditions were agreed upon, and all the plans adjusted. They were upon this wise :—

The British troops—the major part of them already at Long Island—were to be ready, at a moment's notice, to start up the river, while the Americans believed them to be preparing for an expedition to the Chesapeke. All being now agreed upon, André requested that he might be sent back to the *Vulture* in the boat that had brought him ashore. To this, however, Arnold demurred, suggesting his returning by land. Moody and gloomy, possibly beset by doubts as to the success of his scheme, and very likely with a dawning fear of discovery, the safety of his companion seems to have occcupied but a secondary place in his thoughts. He gave him a passport. 'Permit Mr John Anderson to pass the guards to the White Plains or below if he chooses, he being on public business by my orders.—Benedict Arnold.' He then quitted Smith's house, and went up the river himself in safety to his own quarters. The proposed feigned attack by the British on West Point, necessitated their accurate knowledge of its military construction and disposition, so Arnold had supplied André with plans and written particulars·

which the latter was fain to put in his boots for
security.

André had witnessed the compulsory retreat of
the *Vulture* with considerable uneasiness. The boat
by which he had come had been removed from
Haverstraw Creek, but after Arnold's departure,
and towards the evening he tried to induce Smith
to go with him in that or another, to the *Vulture*,
but the latter refused. None being obtainable
without Smith's assistance, he had no alternative
but to go by land, and the latter reluctantly consented to go a part of the way with him. The
question of a change of dress had been strongly
insisted on by Arnold, and Smith endorsed his
opinion, observing that an English officer found
within the American lines would stand a poor chance
of escape. It is almost impossible to believe that
Smith was the dupe he pretended to be, but in any
case the necessities of the position caused resistance
to be useless—indeed, impossible. Accepting, therefore, the inevitable, together with the dress proffered
to him by Smith, André took off his uniform, don-
ning an under-coat of claret colour, a waistcoat and
breeches of nankeen, and the large blue coat over all.
Thus equipped, he started with Smith on his fatal
journey. Their route lay due north by the side of
the river as far as King's Ferry, and here they had
to cross to Verplank on the opposite side, from
thence, east and inland to a place called Pine's Bridge,
and from thence again due south towards New York,

across a large tract of neutral ground which lay
between the latter place and the White Plains.

Accompanied by a negro servant the two started
at sunset on the 21st, having passed the night at
Smith's house. André was thoughtful and silent.
He was fully alive to the dangerous nature of the
journey he had commenced, and could not but
realise that the accomplishment of the undertaking in
which he was playing so active a part was, together
with his life, gravely jeopardised by his compulsory
disobedience to his chief's commands, each one of
which he was most unwillingly transgressing. He
was within the American lines—he had papers of
vital importance in his boots, and he was in a disguised dress. Smith, well acquainted with almost
everyone he met, accosted them all with gay un-
concern. He tried to induce André to talk on indifferent topics, but the latter showed no desire to be
communicative, and thus they crossed the ferry in
moody silence. Arrived at Verplank, they rode
steadily on eastward until nine p.m. when they were
hailed by a sentry and commanded to stop. An
officer, overhearing the challenge, seemed doubtful
about letting them pass, but they produced their
passports and though he professed he was satisfied
he still enquired curiously about their business and
their intentions. He counselled them, moreover, to
go no further that night, and fearful of seeming too
eager to advance, they yielded, and took shelter in a
small house by the roadside. A sleepless night was

André's portion, and at sunrise he got up, and waking the servant they saddled the horses, and offering their host a pecuniary recompense, which he declined, they started afresh for Pine's Bridge.

With the bright morning sun André's spirits rose, and for the rest of the journey he was cheerful and animated, and displayed all the joyousness and charm of manner and conversation for which he was in his own circle renowned. Arrived at Pine's Bridge they breakfasted, and Smith announced his intention of parting with his companion. He divided his money with him, and taking leave of him set out briskly due north towards Fishkill a small town, a few miles beyond Robinson's house, where he had, at Arnold's request, removed his family for a few days during the transactions just recorded. Ten miles' ride brought him to Arnold's quarters, to whom he gave a detailed account of the journey to Pine's Bridge, and then he proceeded to Fishkill.

Meantime André resumed his journey, and for some unexplained reason took a more devious path than he need have done, striking towards the river to Tarrytown, which was but a short distance from the White Plain. The ground near Tarrytown rose on each side of the road, and was covered with trees and bushes, affording a good cover to anyone who desired to conceal themselves. Within but a short distance of what he hoped would be a safe tract of country, and when the sense of danger had nearly passed away, three men sprang suddenly out of the thicket, and down the bank, and seizing the bridle of his horse commanded him to surrender. Extraordinary to relate, he seems to have been taken quite by surprise and from some unaccountable blunder to have believed that his assailants were British. He did not at once produce Arnold's passport, which would have in all probability served its purpose, but by an ill-advised question revealed his nationality. They dragged him from his horse, and on searching him discovered the papers in his boots. He offered them all he had, his watch, his saddle, and bridle, and a hundred guineas, which he would send them if they would release him, but they refused, for he could offer no guarantee for the fulfilment of this last promise. He declined to answer the questions with which they plied him, saying that he would reveal all to any officer before whom they might take him. And now came to light the flaw that premeditated crimes so often contain in their constitution.

The extraordinary carelessness displayed by Arnold in one of the most perilous phases of his treasonable plot, was in direct contrast to the care and trouble he had taken in others. To permit André to carry upon his person, which must, of necessity, be searched in case of accident befalling him, the damning proof of Arnold's own treachery, which could have been easily avoided by making him—André—copy the plans and instructions during his weary day's sojourn at Smith's house, is as incomprehensible as was the action taken by the officer before whom André's captors now

brought him. One Jamieson, was the officer commanding the scouting parties at North Castle, which
was not far from Pine's Bridge, and he seems to have
been—to use a homely phrase—quite bamboozled by
the events thus presented to him for his consideration
and decision. The papers produced and examined
were unquestionably in Arnold's handwriting, the
plans drawn by him, and the explanations certainly
not only written, but endorsed and signed by him.
Every detail concerning the weakness and strength of
the place was described and minutely set forth, and the
particulars of a council of war presided over by Washington (then supposed to be on his way back from his
interview with Rochambeau at Hartford), were fully
reported, and all particulars disclosed and recorded.
Jamieson enclosed these papers to the commander-in-
chief, and despatched them by a messenger, expecting
that the latter would, in all probability, meet him on
the way. He decided that André should be sent with
an escort to Arnold, of all people in the world, but
the reason of this amazing resolution has never been
explained. He wrote Arnold a hasty note, only stating that he sent him one John Anderson, who had
been arrested on his way to New York. ' He had a
passport signed by you,' he said, ' and some papers of
a very dangerous tendency in his stockings ;' adding
that he had sent on all the latter to the commander-
in-chief.

Renewed hope sprang up in André's breast when
he heard what was his destination. Could he gain

M

Robinson's house before the story was published and his capture discovered, Arnold and himself might yet get away to the *Vulture* and avoid the fury of the Americans, for, with a magnanimity unknown to the elder man, no scheme of escape in which Arnold did not bear a share was likely to be considered by André, who now began his journey northwards under the charge of Lieutenant Allen.

Towards evening the second in command, Major Tallmadge, returned to North Castle, and was penetrated with amazement at Jamieson's action, avowing the most decided opinion upon Arnold's guilt, and after much argument and remonstrance he succeeded in inducing Jamieson to despatch another convoy of men after André, to bring him back. Jamieson persisted, however, that the note that he had written to Arnold should proceed, and while André was advancing, in eager and hopeful anticipation of saving both his accomplice and himself, they were overtaken and brought back, while Allen, according to Jamieson's orders, went on with the letter to Robinson's house. André was now transported to Salem, a few miles distant, and when he judged that Arnold had had time to effect his escape, he revealed his real name and status to his captors. By this time, however, Tallmadge had begun to be suspicious of the truth— it was clear the prisoner was a gentleman—and certain movements and habits caused him to believe that he was an officer. Another express was despatched to Washington, giving further details of the

incidents, and André himself wrote a respectful and
dignified letter to the American General. It was
dated September 24th, and expressed a hope that
Washington would believe that he wrote to save himself only from the imputation of having assumed a
mean character for treacherous purposes, and for self-
interest. He avowed his name and military rank.
'The influence of one commander in the army over his
adversary,' said he, 'is an advantage taken in war,'
and a correspondence for this purpose had been held
with Sir Henry Clinton. To this end he—André—
had agreed to meet, upon ground not within the posts
of either army, the one who was to bring them the
intelligence. He himself had been fetched in a boat
from the *Vulture*, and had not been allowed to return.
He was in uniform, and against all stipulations was
conducted without his own knowledge, within the
Americans' lines, and thus—a prisoner—he had to
concert his own escape. He changed his uniform,
he said, and was passed in the night outside the
American posts, and on neutral ground, and was on
his way to New York but was arrested and carried to
Tarrytown, 'and thus I was betrayed,' he added, 'into
the vile condition of an enemy within your posts.'
In dignified terms he added, that though unfortunate
he was branded with nothing dishonourable, and he
could have no motive but that of serving his king. He
was involuntarily an impostor. He asked to be allowed
to send an open letter to his general, and that it
should be taken into consideration that there were

some American officers at Charlestown on parole,
who might be exchanged for him. He brought no
flag,' he concluded, 'and wore his uniform during his
interview with Arnold.' This letter he gave open to
Tallmadge, whose surprise at its contents was extreme.
He was not prepared to hear that the prisoner held
such high military rank. The letter was sealed and
sent on to Washington. André now in a great measure regained his cheerfulness, and though of course
he was strongly guarded, he was treated by the
American officers with the greatest consideration
and courtesy—he, on his part, making the most
favourable impression on all who were brought in
contact with him.

By one of those trifling accidents which sometimes
change a whole history, Washington had resolved
not to return by the same route by which he had
gone to Hartford, but decided to visit the fort at
West Point on his way back. Fulfilling this intention,
he went to Fishkill on the afternoon of the 24th.
There he was unexpectedly detained for the night,
but early next morning he sent off his baggage
and a couple of aides-de-camp to Robinson's house,
bidding them acquaint General Arnold with his
intentions and plans of inspecting West Point, and
saying that he should arrive at Robinson's house to
breakfast. Business detained him however, somewhat longer than he had anticipated, so Arnold and
his guests sat down to the meal. During its progress
a letter was delivered to him—it was that which had

been written by Jamieson and despatched by Allen, and contained the account of André's capture. By a powerful effort Arnold managed to subdue the outward signs of the agitation that overtook him, and although it was apparent to his guests that some untoward incident had come to his knowledge, he was sufficiently master of his countenance and manner to enable him to tell them calmly that his presence was required at West Point, and he requested them to inform Washington on his arrival that he had been summoned thither. He quitted the room and went up to his wife's chamber.

Dauntless in the field, unequalled in resource, and, up to this moment matchless in valour, knowing neither doubt nor fear—having braved death a thousand times—Arnold now cast off his heart of grace together with the last shred of his tarnished honour, and stood before his wife, a pitiable spectacle of naked treachery and demoralised manhood. Realising that one moment's delay might deliver him into the avenging hands of his betrayed and injured compatriots, he had flown into his wife's apartment and there in agitated words and distracted accents, revealed to her so much of the shameful story as could be crushed into an almost momentary interview. To save his own life and to escape the condign vengeance of his comrades he told her he must leave her and fly, and he doubted much whether he should ever see her again. This overwhelming and astounding revelation proved too much for the be-

wildered woman's endurance, and she swooned at his
feet.

Leaving her where she fell, he quitted the apartment dashed down the stair, and, mounting one of
his aides-de-camp's horses that was standing before the
door, rode in headlong haste down the hill to the
river side, and entering a boat caused it to be rowed
out in mid-stream, telling the men that he was going
down the river with a flag, and desired to be back in
time to meet Washington. He urged them down to
King's Ferry, where, displaying a white handkerchief,
he gained the *Vulture*, which was still occupying the
place to which she had moved when André was at
Smith's house. There, we suppose, having told his
story to the captain and Beverley Robinson, together
with the disastrous details of André's capture, and the
consequent collapse of the plot, the ship returned
the same night to New York.

Meanwhile Washington, all unconscious of his
lieutenant's treachery, had eagerly and hopefully laid
his plans for the defeat of the British. His own army
had been reinforced and the French troops were awaiting his orders to join him in the attack upon New
York—the British expedition to the Chesapeke, upon
which the Americans believed or conjectured that the
English were bound—making this, as they thought, a
comparatively easy task.

And now having finished his business at Fishkill, the
American commander-in-chief arrived at Robinson's
house, where he was informed that Arnold had been

hastily summoned to the fort, and entering a barge, he started for West Point, leaving Colonel Hamilton, one of the aides-de-camp, to open any despatches that might arrive. As they crossed over from Robinson's house, it was remarked with some surprise, that the salute that was always fired on the approach of the commander-in-chief was not discharged. An officer received them at the landing-place, and he apologised for the omission, saying they were unaware of his approach. It then transpired that not only was Arnold not in the garrison, but that he had not been there for some days. Washington seemed greatly surprised, but it would appear that his confidence in Arnold was not yet shaken, for he pursued his original intention of inspecting the garrison, a task which occupied several hours. He then returned to Robinson's house, and on landing was met by Colonel Hamilton, who, with dismay in every feature, laid the terrible story before him. Hamilton was despatched on a swift horse to try and discover the traitor's route, but of course several hours' start had placed him in safety. Hamilton, however, met a flag of truce from the *Vulture*, bearing a letter from Arnold to Washington. With the audacity that distinguished him before all others, he solicited protection for his wife and permission for her to return to Philadelphia. 'For himself,' he added, with a presumption that was almost sublime in its amazing assurance, 'he asked no favour, having too often experienced his country's ingratitude. The heart con-

scious of its own rectitude,' he added, 'could not
condescend to palliate its own action.' By the same
means wrote Beverley Robinson, averring that André
came ashore with a flag, on public business, and that
he could not be detained according to the law of nations.
   Nothing could be more ill-advised than such an
appeal. André came ashore with no flag, nor was he
the man to take refuge under the shelter of a lie.
Ignorant to what extent the defection had spread,
Washington took such means as seemed best to get
the troops together in case of an attack on West Point,
and despatching an order to Colonel Jamieson, desired
him to send up the prisoner to Robinson's house under
a strong guard. In due time André arrived, but
Washington from the first refused to see him. He
made many inquiries concerning him, but firmly
declined to permit him to be brought into his presence. He was taken over to West Point, and there
remained till the morning of the 28th when he was
taken in a barge to Stoney Point, and thence, under
an escort of cavalry commanded by Tallmadge, to
Tappan, which was then the head-quarters of Washington's army. No persuasion or pressure could induce André to speak one word that could serve to
implicate anyone but himself. Save in the last act
of merciless expiation or revenge, he was treated with
the utmost consideration by the Americans. A board
of general officers was convened, and he was brought
before them. He spoke with the utmost frankness
and openness, and though he was told that he was not

obliged to answer any question that might implicate himself, he showed neither hesitation nor confusion, comporting himself with dignity and calmness. He denied coming ashore with a flag, adding very truly, that had he done so, he could have returned under its protection. The papers were produced, and he acknowledged that they had been concealed about his person, and he gave a clear and graphic account of the events from the time of his leaving the *Vulture* to the time of his arrest. The examination over, he was asked if he had any remarks to make. He replied, None, but would leave his evidence to operate with the Board. He was then taken back to prison, and after a short consultation the Board reported :—

'First, that he came ashore from the *Vulture* in the night, in a private and secret manner; Secondly, that he changed his dress within our lines and under a feigned name, and in a disguised habit, passed our works at Stoney and Verplank Points, was taken at Tarrytown in this disguised habit, being on his way to New York, and when taken had in his possession papers containing information for the enemy.' They farther reported, 'that, in their opinion, Major André should be treated as a spy and should suffer death.'

'Never, perhaps,' says Colonel Hamilton in a letter to a friend, 'did a man suffer death with more justice, or deserve it less.' He visited him several times in his prison, and was greatly impressed by his composure, dignity and obvious loyalty. André talked calmly and without bitterness of his position.

' I foresee my fate,' said he, 'and although I do not pretend to act the part of a hero, or to be indifferent to life, yet I am reconciled to whatever may happen, conscious that misfortune and not guilt has brought it on me. Sir Henry Clinton has been too good to me, he has been lavish of his kindness. I am bound to him by too many obligations, and love him too much to bear the thought that he should reproach himself on the supposition of my having conceived myself obliged, by his instructions, to run the risk I did.' Struggling with his emotion, and unable entirely to repress his tears, he added : ' I wish to be allowed to assure him I did not act under this impression, but submitted to a necessity imposed upon me, as contrary to my own inclinations as to his orders.'

His request was at once granted, and the following is the copy of the letter that he wrote to the British commander-in-chief :—

' SIR,—Your Excellency is doubtless apprised of the manner in which I was taken, and possibly of the serious light in which my conduct is considered, and the rigorous determination that is impending. Under these circumstances, I have obtained General Washington's permission to send you this letter, the object of which is to remove from your breast any suspicion that I could imagine that I was bound by your Excellency's orders to expose myself to what has happened. The events of coming within an enemy's post, and of changing my dress, which led me to my present situation, were contrary to my own intentions, as they were to your orders, and the circuitous route which I took was imposed—perhaps unavoidably—without alternative upon me. I am perfectly tranquil in mind and prepared for any fate to which an honest zeal for my king's service may have devoted me.

'In addressing myself to your Excellency on this occasion, the force of all my obligations to you, and of the attachment and gratitude I bear to you, recurs to me, and I send you the most earnest wishes for your welfare which a faithful, affectionate and respectful attendant can frame.

'I have a mother and two sisters to whom the value of my commission would be an object, as the loss of Granada has much affected their income. It is needless to be more explicit on this subject, I am persuaded of your Excellency's goodness. I receive the greatest attention from General Washington, and from every person under whose charge I happen to be placed.—I have the honour to be, with the most respectful attachment, your Excellency's most obedient and most humble servant,—JOHN ANDRÉ, *D. Adj.-Gen.*'

The account of the proceedings of the Board were sent, together with letter, to Sir Henry, who received the news of his young aide-de-camp's fate with the utmost grief and dismay. He wrote to Washington telling him that all the circumstances had not been laid before him, and beseeching him to send someone to represent him under a flag of truce, to meet his—

Sir Henry's—delegates, who would make certain representations to him, together with facts and details
unknown to him. Washington consented, and the
execution, which was to have taken place on the 1st,
was postponed for the purpose. The meeting took
place at Dobbs' Ferry, and lasted for several hours.
Clinton sent Beverley Robinson—a not very judicious selection as it seems to us—and two general
officers besides, but only Robinson was permitted
to advance. General Greene represented Washington.
Beverley Robinson was so well satisfied with the
apparent impression on the delegates that he avowed
to Clinton his belief in the success of his mission.

Robinson was also the bearer of a letter to Washington from Arnold, which was of so extraordinary a nature
that it seems impossible to believe that it was written
in good faith, and which Robinson should have
refused to transmit. Arnold screened André from all
blame, but as he himself was safe under the protection
of the British flag, there was not much magnanimity
in the avowal. 'If,' said this arch-traitor, 'after this
just and candid representation of the case, the Board
adheres to their views, I shall suppose it dictated by
passion and resentment, and if André should suffer
the severity of the sentence, I shall think myself
bound, by every tie of duty and honour, to retaliate on
such unhappy persons as may fall within my power
in your army, so that the respect due to flags and the
law of nations may be better respected and observed ;
if this warning be disregarded and he suffer, I call

heaven and earth to witness that your Excellency will be answerable for the torrent of blood that may be spilt in consequence.'

If any circumstance bearing upon so disastrous and deplorable an event could be termed ludicrous, this letter, so exasperating in its inconceivable effrontery and insolent, vulgar egotism, may be so called. Washington was we believe, incapable of permitting a perfidious knave's words to influence his decision—one that we believe had been taken from the first—and certainly threats and objurgations are not usually successful when applied to a man like the American commander-in-chief. The sentence therefore remained unrescinded, and was to be carried into execution on the morrow. The manner of his death afflicted André at least as much as the fact, and he made one more effort to induce Washington to substitute the death of shooting for that of hanging in the following letter :—

'TAPPAN, *Oct. 1st*, 1780.

'SIR,—Buoyed above the terror of death, by the consciousness of a life devoted to honourable pursuits, and stained with no action that can give me remorse, I trust that the request that I make to your Excellency at this serious period, and which is to soften my last moments, will not be rejected.

'Sympathy towards a soldier will surely induce your Excellency and a military tribunal to adapt the mode of my death to the feelings of a man of honour. Let me hope, sir, that if aught in my character im-

presses you with esteem towards me as the victim of
policy and not of resentment, I shall experience the
operation of these feelings by being informed that I
am not to die on a gibbet.—I have the honour to be
your Excellency's most obedient and most humble
servant,   'JOHN ANDRÉ,
'*D. Adjutant-General to the British Army.*'

That there is a time when forbearance, ceasing to
be a virtue, degenerates into weakness is a truism, and
it is only the highest minded men who can preserve
under trying circumstances, the balance of mind necessary to form a correct judgment as to when this point
has been reached.   The dire calamity of the betrayal
of West Point, only checked on the very brink of its
execution, would have been largely owing to Washington's obstinate, perverse and unreasonable belief in one
who had covered himself with shame and dishonour ;
and this ought rather to have influenced his actions
towards mercy, but he could not, at anyrate he did not,
separate the actions of the two men.   Doubtless he
would have preferred that Arnold should suffer, but as
he had made good his escape, his relentless vengeance
fell on André.   But had the latter's prayer been granted,
and a *soldier's* death been substituted for a malefactor's,
Washington's reputation would not have suffered, and
the chivalrous nation which he represented, would
assuredly have endorsed an act of grace and mercy,
rather than one of revenge and cruelty.

André was confined in what was called 'the old

Dutch Church,' a small stone building with only one door. He was closely guarded by six sentinels. On the morning of the execution he showed no emotion. Permission had been granted for his servant to bring him linen and clothes from New York. While the man was attending upon him he burst into tears. 'Leave me,' said André, 'till you can command yourself, and then return.' He was perfectly calm and composed. Breakfast was served him from Washington's table, and he conversed cheerfully with the officers who were with him. 'I am ready, gentlemen,' said he, when the hour struck, and, rising from his chair, he prepared to leave the room.

It was high noon when the door of the prison-house was thrown open and the prisoner stepped across the threshold into the bright sunshine of the still, October day. He was attired in the uniform of a British major, his bearing was erect and noble, and there was neither trepidation nor anxiety in his aspect. No passing stranger could have surmised—save from the sorrowful looks of the multitudes who had assembled to witness the tragic end of the brave young English officer, the fame of whose misfortunes, youth and gallant bearing had spread already amongst the people—that he was marching direct into the expectant jaws of death, and as he descended the outside stair to take his place in the procession, every breath was held, and a silence, oppressive in its solemnity, reigned over all, while the sympathy of the whole concourse went out to him with a rush that was

almost tangible. A detachment of 300 soldiers formed
the escort, and were placed in single file on each side
of the road. The procession was headed by a large
number of American officers, all of the highest rank,
and on horseback, Washington alone conspicuous by
his absence. The waggon containing the coffin came
next, jolting noisily along the rough and stony road.
Immediately behind came a group of American officers,
André in their midst. As he marched along between
Tallmadge and another, he saluted all the officers with
whom he was acquainted, smiling and bowing, especially noticing those who had composed the Board.
'By heaven,' said Tallmadge, 'I never saw a man I so
pitied, he had the greatest accomplishments—he was
Sir Henry's Prime Minister. He has told me all his
motives, and is as cheerful as if going to an assembly.
I walked to the scaffold with him, and parted from him
beneath it, overwhelmed with grief that so gallant an
officer and so accomplished a gentleman should come
to such an end.' Slowly the procession wound up the
rising ground, at the top of which was a field without
any enclosure, and here had been erected a very high
gallows. When this first came in view André started
back, showing for the first time symptoms of discom-
posure. 'I am reconciled to my death but not to its
mode,' he said, in answer to Tallmadge's sympathetic
glance. Although he had received no reply from Washington, he had believed that the boon preferred with so
much unconscious dignity and pathos would have been
granted, but Washington's stern and uncompromising

mood knew neither pity nor remorse. The General
Order of Execution was then read, and at its conclusion André uncovered and bowed.

The waggon containing the coffin was drawn under-
neath the gallows.

'I observed some trepidation,' said a spectator, 'as,
while standing there, he placed his foot on a stone,
rolling it over, while there was a slight choking in his
throat.'

'It will be but a momentary pang,' he said a
moment after, as he lifted his head, and, placing his
hand on the back part of the waggon, he vaulted
lightly in, and, stepping on to his coffin, divested
himself of his hat and coat. He then drew forth two
handkerchiefs, bound his eyes, adjusted the noose
himself, and handing the other one to the execu-
tioner, submitted himself to him while he tied his
hands behind his back.

The commanding officer asked him if he had anything to say.

'I pray you to bear witness,' he replied simply,
'that I die as a brave man should.'

His hair, according to the fashion of the day, was
bound with a black ribbon, which heightened his
youthful appearance. The waggon was then withdrawn quickly, and André expiated the crimes of
others with his life. His body remained hanging for
half an hour amid the awestruck silence of the
multitude.

'No chamber of death,' said a spectator, 'was ever
N

stiller than the surroundings of the scaffold during
that time.'

A grave was dug immediately beneath. He was
cut down, and the body laid on the ground. His
servant helped to put him in his coffin, and he was
buried on the spot, a small fir-tree and a heap of
stones marking the place.

Reluctantly we now turn to finish the story of
Arnold's dishonoured career.

In consequence of some extraordinary obliquity of
judgment, some impossibility in his mental powers to
recognise his true position in relation to honest men, he
actually sent in his formal resignation to Washington,
requesting him to lay it before Congress, intimating
that *he would never serve them any more, nor need they
expect it.* When the letter was shown to Greene, he
flung it from him with an indignation he could not
repress. Arnold also addressed the people of America
in a long and insolent letter, which, to notice seriously,
would have conferred on the writer an importance, it
is idle to observe, he had forfeited a thousand times
over. According to the agreement with Clinton, he
was made a brigadier-general, and the sum of £6000
was bestowed upon him. Clinton must have found
him a very embarrassing possession, and one that, in
spite of his capacities, he would gladly have been rid
of. Rewards were offered by the Americans for his
capture, and a project devised to kidnap him and
bring him to justice. Washington sanctioned the
scheme, only stipulating that he was to be brought

to him alive. Unfortunately the plan failed. The authorities of Pennsylvania required at this time that Mrs Arnold should quit the state in fourteen days, and she rejoined her husband in New York. The populace had burned him in effigy, but with a chivalry that cannot be too highly commended, she passed through their midst with no hostile demonstration against herself or her husband.

Clinton employed Arnold on an expedition to Virginia, but two men were commissioned to watch him that he did not betray our arms.

'What,' he once asked of an American prisoner, 'would be my fate if I were captured by your army?'

'Your fate!' replied the officer. 'Why, they would cut off the leg that was injured at Quebec and Saratoga and hang the rest of you on a gibbet.'

His familiarity with the country caused him to be employed on several occasions. He commanded the expedition to New London, his native place, and was the instrument of its destruction by fire. It was even said that he watched the burning of the city from the belfry of a steeple. Reviled and execrated by his fellow-countrymen, he was naturally regarded by the English with distrust and scorn.

In December 1781 he sailed, with his family, to England, the war being at an end. Some say that he was made much of at the British Court, and it is true that a pension was granted to his wife. The king and a few others took a certain amount of notice of him, but he was avoided and shunned by almost all. In

the House of Lords the Earl of Lauderdale, in a speech
on a government appointment to which he was taking
exception on the grounds of the recipient changing sides,
said—'If apostacy can justify promotion,' said he, 'he
is the most fit person for the command, General Arnold alone excepted.' Arnold happened to be present,
and sent him a challenge. A meeting followed, in
which Charles James Fox acted as Lauderdale's second.
Lauderdale received Arnold's fire, and then contemp-
tuously discharged his pistol in the air, refusing either
explanation or apology ; but the matter was somehow patched up and they left the ground. In 1794
he went to the West Indies on some commercial business. In 1798 all England was arming against France,
and he addressed an appeal to the Duke of York to
be employed on active service, but his petition was refused, and in bitterness of spirit he at length realised,
that from out such depths of baseness as he had fallen
there was no resurrection. He fitted out some privateers to fight against France, but was a large loser
by the speculation. He became restless, nervous,
irritable, sank into bad health and died in London, on
14th June 1801, in poverty and distress.

In the autumn of 1821, in consequence of the
representations made by the British Consul at New
York to the home government about the indifference
and disrespect shown to the memory of the officers
who had died for their country, André's remains were
exhumed, and transmitted to England for interment
in Westminster Abbey. Mr Buchanan the Consul

superintended their removal, and an interesting account of the circumstances was published shortly
after. On a hill commanding a magnificent view
of the surrounding country, and of that portion of
it that was occupied by Washington's troops in 1780,
they had little difficulty in finding the grave where the
young hero had rested undisturbed for forty-one years.
The ground was so situated that the tragedy there
enacted must have been fully visible to Washington
and his soldiers from their quarters. The field had
been cultivated, but the plough had spared the grave,
the place of which was marked by two pine-trees,
and a lady had planted a peach-tree at its head.
Though so many years had elapsed since the events
recorded, the story and fame of André's gallantry and
misfortune, his youth and his chivalry still lingered
amongst the country people, and many from the
surrounding villages accompanied the Englishman
as he went up the hill to execute his mission. The
work of excavation was commenced, and the spades of
the workmen soon struck upon the coffin, the lid of
which was found to be broken. With great care it was
removed, and under the eyes of the sympathetic be-
holders lay all that remained of the bright and gallant
young André. The roots of the peach-tree had
pierced the coffin and completely surrounded his
skull like a net—his uniform had been taken away
by his servant on the day of his death, and there was
only left a portion of his fair and boyish hair, together
with the mouldering ribbon that had tied it on the

day of his execution. All those assembled passed by in regular order to view the remains which were reverently collected and placed in a sarcophagus which had been provided for the purpose, and which was then carried to the pastor's house, there to await its removal to New York, and thence to the ship that was to convey them to England. The hair and ribbon were sent to his sisters, and the peach-tree, which had been uprooted, was planted in the garden of Carlton House. King George III., ever mindful of the claims of those who served their country with fidelity, and their sovereign with loyalty, had been deeply moved at the ignominious death of the brave and unfortunate young soldier—a death, however, whose ignominy was transformed into glory and renown by his brave simplicity and inherent courage. King George also bestowed a baronetcy on his next brother, who dying without children, the title became extinct.

Many of those who have wandered in the aisles of Westminster Abbey musing upon the wealth of greatness, honour, and fame that lies there enshrined, are acquainted with the monument that was placed there by his king to the memory of as dauntless a spirit, and gallant a gentleman, as sleeps even in that time-honoured and hallowed spot.

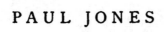

PAUL JONES

PAUL JONES

CHAPTER I

IT is curious how very few of this generation have any knowledge of the history of Paul Jones. A naval commander of no small attainments, of extraordinary resolution and splendid courage, his name, with the fame of which only a hundred years ago both the New and the Old World rang, has died away, till it has become but an echo of past times.

A Scotchman by birth, an American by choice, and a buccaneer in feeling, he served under more than one flag with the distinction that such qualities as his must always command. The brilliancy of his deeds, however, was dimmed by the grave and weighty imperfections of character that constantly marred his career as a successful commander. The place in history that has been allotted to him is that of a pirate and adventurer; and though he fairly earned the latter designation, it is doubtful whether he should be classed with the former, inasmuch as he at no period sailed without a properly authorised commission from the country in whose service he fought at the time.

The only act that can justly fall under the category of piracy was his extraordinary and impudent descent on St Mary's Isle, the seat of the Earl of Selkirk—a proceeding which, in spite of all that has been written in its defence, even by the victims themselves, appears to have been one of blustering vanity, condoned quite unaccountably by the persons chiefly concerned, as may be seen by Lord Selkirk's inconceivably acquiescent and even laudatory reply to Paul's bombastic and ridiculous effusion, written more in explanation of than in excuse for his plunderous visit.

Paul Jones was born in 1747 at Arbigland, in the parish of Kirkbean, in Kirkcudbright. He was the fifth son of John Paul, a native of Fife, who was a gardener in the service of Mr Craig of Arbigland.

Why he assumed the name of Jones appears to be doubtful, but he adopted it pretty early in his career. Born and bred by the sea, he imbibed that passionate desire for a sailor's life that has shaped the course of many brave men, and at twelve years old he was bound apprentice to Mr Younger, of Whitehaven, who owned a trading vessel called the *Friendship*. In this he made his first voyage to Rappahannock in Virginia, and on the shores of this river he landed, having a brother a settler there, and with him while the *Friendship* remained in port, he lived.

In the course of a short time Mr Younger's affairs

became embarrassed, and this led to Paul's indentures being cancelled. Released from his obligations, he obtained the appointment of third mate on board the *King George*, of Whitehaven, a vessel belonging to the slave-trade. From this he, in 1766, passed into the brigantine *Two Friends*, engaged in the same traffic. The intervals of leisure he employed in studying the different branches of his profession. He states that he quitted the *Two Friends* on account of his hatred for the cruelties practised in the business, and he returned to Scotland in 1768.

On this voyage it happened that both the captain and the mate died of fever, and there being no one on board so capable of navigating the ship, Paul assumed the command, bringing her safely into port.

So well satisfied were her owners with the skill and judgment he had displayed, that they at once appointed him master and supercargo. It was on board this vessel that an incident occurred of which there are several accounts. What appears to be the truth is, that the ship's carpenter, one Mungo Maxwell, was so severely punished by Paul for some trivial offence that he died. It is reported that soon after this event he engaged in the smuggling trade; but he always denied this with an indignation which, considering all things, seems superfluous.

Afterwards he obtained the command of the *Betsey*, of London, a West Indian trader; and he remained for some time in those islands, engaged in commercial speculations, which were probably successful, as he is

said to have been possessed of considerable funds in
Tobago. He remained for about a year and a half
unoccupied as regards the active part of his profession,
but probably employing his time in educating himself;
for in those days the son of a working man, and moreover one who went to sea at twelve years old as a
cabin-boy, could hardly have attained to the pro-
ficiency of Paul Jones' style of writing without more
learning than could be had at a parish school; for
though his phraseology is boastful and ridiculous to
excess, it is certainly not that of an illiterate man, and
it displays considerable power of description.

The revolt of the American colonies was at this
time (1775) in full progress—political feeling ran very
high; but whether Paul really embraced the principles
he so loudly applauded, or whether—which appears at
least as likely—he saw his way to distinction more
surely by denouncing the land of his birth, is a moot
point.

At anyrate, Paul, now twenty-eight years old,
watched, with growing interest and anxiety, the ever-
increasing bitterness of the struggle between the two
countries, and no sooner saw that the contending
parties were coming to blows at sea, than he threw in
his part with the rebellious colony, and was—when
the time came that his name became famous throughout the world—very naturally branded by England as
a rebel and a traitor.

' I was indeed born in Britain,' he wrote some years

later, 'but I do not inherit the degenerate spirit of that fallen nation, which I at once lament and despise. It is far beneath me to reply to their hireling invective. They are strangers to the inward approbation that greatly animates and rewards the man who draws his sword only in support of the dignity of freedom. America has been the country of my fond election from the age of thirteen, when I first saw it. I had the honour to hoist, with my own hands, the flag of freedom the first time it was displayed, and I have attended it with veneration ever since on the ocean.'

Such loud reiterations of high motives and disinterested zeal in the cause of liberty, such ostentatious asseverations of purity of principle, might cast doubt on the sincerity of men far above Paul Jones in the moral scale.

Joseph Hawes, a member of the newly-formed Marine Committee of the United States, appears to have befriended him at this time, and thus patronised he entered the American service. His capabilities had been, in all likelihood, pretty shrewdly gauged, and they assuredly proved, in many ways, of great advantage to the infant navy then struggling for existence.

His first commission, dated December 1775, was that of first lieutenant to the *Alfred*, then lying before Philadelphia ; and it was on board this ship that Paul Jones, with his own hands, hoisted the Stars and Stripes for the first time in the naval history of the States—

the flag under which he fought with so much valour and success.

The whole of the American naval armament consisted at this time of five ships of sorts, and though there was much difficulty in obtaining the services of properly qualified officers even for these, thirteen other frigates had been, in view of the coming struggles, ordered to be built. This adventurous and presumptuous little fleet was put under the command of a man named Hopkins, whose merits do not appear to have been great.

Paul was restrained by no respect for the commander-in-chief; and the voyage, which was made for the purpose of harassing British ships, was a series of quarrels, recriminations, accusations, and retaliation between the two. Paul was unquestionably the more capable of the two men, but discipline was the last virtue dreamt of by him as regarded his own relations with the commander-in-chief, and this latter was either not invested with the necessary power to quell his rebellious subordinate, or lacked the necessary decision.

Paul, however, cherished the strictest and most severe opinions relative to naval discipline as regarded others, and his own behaviour is a ludicrous example of his overweening and extravagant opinion of his own merits.

Every one of these expeditions, which lasted from 1776 to 1778, was marred by his disputes with the commander-in-chief. Each party complained to the Marine Committee, who strove to smooth matters over with the least possible injury to the pride of both ; but the condition of the navy must have been almost chaotic, for Hopkins not only acted, as regarded Jones, independently of the Marine Committee, but these last reappointed him to fresh commands as fast as Hopkins superseded him, while the object of so much discussion heeded no one's will but his own. In the intervals of employment he gave himself up to the study of modelling and organising the navy, urging upon the authorities, as before mentioned, the strictest discipline as indispensable for its successful develop-ment, and also suggesting the adoption of the examina-tion system to secure properly qualified officers for the service, besides the formation of a Board of Admiralty to adjudicate in all naval matters.

His energetic appeals to Congress had their due effect. No officer, in spite of serious faults, had shown such ability and courage as Paul had ; and as diffid-ence formed no part of his character, he duly im-pressed the fact on the authorities ; and so, after endless correspondence, innumerable appeals, and several visits to Boston, he was appointed to a ship called the *Ranger* at the end of 1777.

America had declared her independence in 1776, and hostilities between the two nations continued with ever-growing bitterness. The British arms had met with many defeats on land in America; while the maladministration of the navy, with Lord Sandwich as First Lord, had been the cause of grave and omin-ous occurrences at sea.

While these events were agitating Great Britain, Dr Franklin, Silas Deane, and Arthur Lee had been publicly received at the French Court as ambassadors and commissioners from the United States ; and Paul Jones, in the *Ranger*, slipped across the Atlantic, bearing with him a letter from Congress to the ambassadors at Versailles, charging them to give him the command of a frigate, the *Indien*, then built at Amsterdam for their service.

Arrived at the port of Nantes, he was at once summoned to Versailles, the object being to concert with him a plan of operations for the maritime force of the Comte d'Estaing ; for although war had not been declared between England and France, the two nations were in a state of smouldering hostility—and while indirectly supporting the cause of America, France eagerly desired to harass and damage the British fleet. He received his final instructions from the commissioners, and sailed to Quiberon, where, after some altercation and objections raised by the French admiral, this latter was compelled to salute the American flag.

Paul had been the first to unfurl it, and by his firmness and address he was thus the means of establishing its place among the nations. It must be acknowledged that he had some reason to be proud. For some time Paul had cherished, among other audacious schemes, to be alluded to hereafter, a favourite one for the destruction of Whitehaven. He had passed much of his time there when in the service of English

traders, and probably had many friends and acquaintances among the inhabitants. This consideration does
not, however, appear to have had the least influence
in hindering him in his purpose. Franklin's orders
were discretionary and unlimited, and he acted entirely in accordance with the dictates of his own will.
Vanity being his ruling passion, he was presumably
actuated as much by the desire of flaunting his name
and deeds before the eyes of those who, so far from
having injured him, had done him many an act of
kindness in the days of his boyhood, as by the wish to
revenge the British cruelties perpetrated in America.

Between the coasts of England and Ireland he
hovered for some days. Wind and weather were
boisterous and unsuitable for his project. He had
come out of the harbour of Brest on the 10th April,
and it was not until the 21st that, beating about
Carrickfergus, he descried a ship lying at anchor in
the roads. A fishing-boat coming alongside the
Ranger, he detained it, and ascertained that the vessel
in question was the *Drake,* an English war-ship of
twenty guns. The weather increasing in turbulence
forced Paul to run for shelter under the south coast
of Scotland; but on the 22d it faired, and midnight
found him lying-to before Whitehaven.

Having laid his plans, he despatched one boat with
ten volunteers and two officers with combustibles, and
orders to set fire to the ships lying in the harbour on
the north side of the pier—he himself commanded
another boat and party, and landed on the south side

O

in order to secure the fort. Scaling the wall, he crept
through one of the embrasures, and stealthily arrived
at the guard-room, inside which the sentinels were
profoundly sleeping. Promptly locking them in, he
spiked all the guns in the fort, and hurrying round to
the other side, joined the other boat's crew.

By some means or other one of the men—an
Englishman named Freeman—probably conscience-
stricken at finding himself engaged in an incendiary
expedition against his own countrymen, contrived to
escape, and ran down Marlborough Street, knocking
at the doors as he went, to rouse the inhabitants and
give the alarm, bidding them wake, for the shipping
was being fired and the town would soon be in flames.
Meantime Paul arrived on the quay only to find that
his men had failed to carry out his instructions.
Hastily placing a guard over the ship he designed to
fire, he procured a light from a house close by, and
dashing back to the quay and on board the vessel,
kindled it in the steerage.

By this time day was beginning to break; and the
inhabitants, who had been terrified by Freeman's
shouts, came crowding down to the quay where 'I
stood,' says Paul, in his subsequent account to the
commissioners, and with his accustomed swaggering
mendaciousness, 'between them and the ship, pistol
in hand, and ordered them to retire, which they did
precipitately; the flames caught the rigging, and we
re-embarked.'

Had this account even approached the truth, nothing could have saved the shipping in the harbour. Over one hundred and twenty ships—nearly three hundred, says Paul himself—lying one against the other at low tide, unsurrounded by water, could not have escaped had the rigging of one of them, as he asserted, caught fire, and had the inhabitants, as he states, been prevented from extinguishing the flames. ' I stood alone on the pier,' he proceeds, ' and gazed at the amazed inhabitants, who dared not attempt to extinguish the flames.' His departure from White-haven, he would have had the world believe, resembled the transformation-scene of a modern pantomime ; for he retired, by his own account, wrapped in a blaze of splendour and illumined by the flames of the burn-ing ships, whereas the prosaic truth is that he failed in a dastardly attack on the home of his youth, and a considerable doubt arises in reading his boastful narrative as to whether his own retreat was not as hasty as he described the ' precipitate retirement' of the Whitehaveners. Thoroughly unsuccessful in their undertaking, Paul and his men made the best of their way back to the *Ranger*.

In the despatch in which he relates the details of this affair, Paul accounts for his failure—which he has, at all events, partially to acknowledge, inasmuch as he could not assert that the town was burnt—by com-plaining of the backwardness of some of those under his command, and explains, with much detail, how it would certainly have been laid in ashes but for this cause. He assigns, in that document, as a reason for his attack upon Whitehaven, the outrages on America of which the English had been guilty, adding that his object was an exchange of prisoners in Europe, and to stop ' by one good fire ' the British cruelties.

How the commissioners received this rodomontade we are not told.

His vanity was to receive ample amends in his next adventure. Sailing away from Whitehaven in the early morning of the 24th, he wended his way towards Scotland, and entered the Solway Firth. Whether the extraordinary act that followed was the result of a resolution long made, or whether it was the impulse of the moment, does not appear.

A raid upon a solitary country house, dependent upon its own inhabitants for its protection, is not, however, a very valorous or chivalrous deed, nor one that can inspire anyone with admiration for its gallantry, or indeed with any feeling but surprise at its audacity.

Owing to the situation of St Mary's Isle, the seat of the Earl of Selkirk, which is a peninsula at low tide, and an island at high tide, he was obliged to lay to at Little Ross, a mile from the house. Twenty-six men entered the longboat of the *Ranger*, and Paul, delegating the command to Lieutenant Simpson, accompanied them himself to the extremity of St Mary's Isle, where they landed, Paul remaining with the boat. The house stands below the town, amid the lands which are flooded at high tide.

The marauders stepped ashore at once. They had

received orders to seize Lord Selkirk's person, and carry him back with them. Passing by the gardens, they met several of the *employés*, and although the appearance of so large a body of men created some surprise, no one seems to have experienced any alarm, the impression being that it was a press-gang party, and for this reason they probably gave them a wide berth. Arrived before the house, the word of command was given to surround it, and to keep a sharp look-out, and the two officers advanced to the entrance to announce their intentions. Somewhat nonplused by the information given them by the servant, that Lord Selkirk was in London, they requested to see Lady Selkirk, adding that they had important business with her.

Apprehending no danger, Lady Selkirk desired that they should be ushered into a chamber on the ground-floor, and at once joined them. She had evidently adopted the same opinion as the people who met them on their way, and assumed that their object was to press men. She did not believe, she said, that they would find anyone on the island suitable for their purpose. Upon this the officers threw back their surtouts, displaying the American uniform of green coats, faced with white, and trimmed with silver braid, saying it was no longer needful to conceal their purpose, for they were no press-gang, but officers belonging to the ship *Ranger*, commanded by Paul Jones. Their orders, they said, were to carry off Lord Selkirk ; but as he was absent—and this was probably an inspiration of the moment—they should requisition all the plate, and their orders must be executed forthwith.

Quick as thought Lady Selkirk realised the situation, and seeing how useless must be any resistance to so formidable a band of men, she, with infinite dignity and perfect calm, consented at once. She trusted, she said, that no insult would be offered to herself or any of her household. To this the officers replied, that provided they were obeyed, they had orders only to surround the house, and permit no one to leave it. Lady Selkirk quietly gave the necessary instructions, while the officers, with the arrogant flourish always adopted by Paul, and probably acquired from him by his subordinates, assured her that they did not regret Lord Selkirk's absence, as their captain knew him well, and had a high opinion of him. It seems strange that this patronising view of his character expressed by one known as a rebel and execrated as a pirate, should have done ought but anger Lord Selkirk when he came to learn these strange events.

Paul left the paternal roof at twelve years of age, and appears to have returned there no more till he burst like a bomb on the unoffending mansion of his father's master; but it will be seen that Lord Selkirk not only condoned, but indirectly acquiesced in, the act of robbery described.

I have seen no description of this doughty deed in Paul's own words, but there is a letter addressed by him to Lady Selkirk on his arrival at Brest, whither he went a day or two later, and after his battle with the *Drake* the following day. There is also that which he addressed to Lord Selkirk six years later, on the occasion of the restoration of the plate, together with Lord Selkirk's reply. The first is dated May 1778, and speaks in bombastic terms of his raid on St Mary's Isle, and alludes to himself as a 'man of fine feelings and real sensibility,' and to the act itself as one of which he disapproved, but had been forced into, in spite of himself; while he adds that his desire was, by means of his abduction, to make Lord Selkirk the 'happy instrument' of alleviating the miseries of the American prisoners—a wish which it is highly improbable that Lord Selkirk shared. In flowery language he recounts the previous day's events at Whitehaven, and finishes a ridiculous and fulsome eulogy on Lady Selkirk by pointing out his own forbearance and consideration, announcing that his seamen had 'accepted the plate offered' in lieu of Lord Selkirk's person, and adding, with the only genuine touch of nature in the whole fanfaronade, a reproach that the quantity fell far short of that expressed in the inventory.

The next, six years later, he wrote to Lord Selkirk concerning its restoration, and explaining why it had not been returned sooner. Although it is not likely that Lord Selkirk desired at any time to be a vicarious sufferer in anyone's behalf, he wrote Paul a letter, 'which,' says his biographer naively, and apparently

with the fullest confidence in the buccaneer's veracity,
'was some indemnity for his trouble and anxiety.'
Lord Selkirk replied by apologetically explaining the
reason of the delay in answering, but says that, though
the plate met with delays, it had at last arrived, and
that he had intended putting in the newspapers a high
testimonial regarding the behaviour of Paul's men on
the memorable occasion.

The cheerful acceptance of and amiable acquiescence
in the views set forth in Paul's bombastic effusions
baffle comprehension and exhaust patience. Paul's
letter to Lady Selkirk is perhaps the most presumptuous (and successful) attempt to account for an impudent robbery, by claiming chivalrous motives, on
record—moreover, it carries falsehood on its face.

The plate was requisitioned on finding that the
object of their search was absent—Paul was not on
the spot, moreover, therefore that he carried off the
plate against his will and to alleviate his men's discontent is clearly untrue. He besides expressed his
disappointment that there was so small a quantity of
the booty, and it is a fact that, but for the insistence
of Franklin, it would not have been restored at all.
The latter was doubtless unwilling that such an act
of piracy should stain the American cause.

It is somewhat difficult to understand that such a
deed—even though effected without violence, a result
due to Lady Selkirk's courage and presence of mind
alone—should excite the warm feelings of almost
apologetic admiration and gratitude that appear to

have animated Lord Selkirk's breast, and dictated his reply when he wrote to acknowledge the receipt of the plate—absent without leave for six years. If Paul had a sense of humour, he must have been infinitely amused at being taken so exactly at his own valuation.

We must now go back to the *Ranger*, which immediately on the return of Paul and his band, who, of course, carried with them the spoils of their adventure set sail for the Irish Coast. Arriving in Belfast Lough, they found the *Drake*, the object of their quest, preparing to come out of Carrickfergus. 'No time,' says a contemporary account, 'could have been more unfortunate for the *Drake* for such an encounter. Captain Burdon was up in years, and very ill at the time; the lieutenant and boatswain had just died, and no one had as yet replaced them.'

Lieutenant Dobbs had just been appointed to the *Defiance*, but happening to be at Belfast, and seeing the dilemma in which Captain Burdon was placed, gallantly went off to the *Drake* as she was in the act of quitting the harbour.

The *Drake*, as she neared the *Ranger*, hoisted the British colours; the *Ranger* responded with the Stars and Stripes. The *Drake* then hailed, demanding what ship she was. The *Ranger's* reply was a broadside, and the battle began.

The sun was just setting over Carrickfergus when the *Ranger's* guns thundered forth their challenge. For sixty-five minutes, during which period the contest lasted, the *Drake* made the most gallant and strenuous efforts to overcome the superior strength of the enemy. Long before the end Burdon was entreated to yield and strike, but he refused, and continued the struggle with the most obstinate courage until a musket shot killed him on the spot. Without a moment's delay, Lieutenant Dobbs sprang to the place of the fallen captain and promptly assumed the command, but in a very short time he too fell mortally wounded, and was carried below, only to die in a few hours.

Meantime the rigging was shot away, the ship entirely disabled, and darkness fell upon the scene as the *Ranger*, master of the situation, finished her work. And so the gallant *Drake* struck her colours, and Paul Jones was victor. Three fishermen of Carrickfergus were on board the *Ranger* during the action. Six men had come out in response to Paul's signals for a pilot. He sent three back, but he detained the other three. At the conclusion of the fight he sent them ashore in a boat belonging to the *Drake*, bidding them '*take a piece of the mainsail to the Governor to make him a pair of trousers.*' Paul states his losses to have been two officers and eight men, and the following day he re-entered Brest harbour, after an absence of twenty-eight days.

It is worthy of record that Lieutenant Dobbs had only been married three days when he so gallantly volunteered, and fell during his patriotic act of duty. He was a native of Lisburn, near Belfast, and the

following inscription was placed on a marble tablet
in the church :—

'This Marble is sacred to the memory of Lieutenant William Dobbs, a naval officer, who terminated
his career of virtue by an illustrious display of valour
on board one of his Majesty's Sloops of War, while
endeavouring to snatch victory from fortune in opposition to superior force.   He fell, a self-devoted victim
to his country.   His body rests in that element on
which Great Britian has long rode triumphant by the
exertions of men like him.   His afflicted fellow-towns-
men, by strewing laurels over his empty monument,
do honour to themselves—they can add nothing to
his fame.   He was born at Lisburn, on 22d day of
September 1746, and died of his wounds on board the
Drake, April 26th, 1778.'

CHAPTER II

PAUL JONES, roving unchecked about our own home
seas, could not have been a very edifying spectacle for
patriotic Englishmen, and none the more that the
hero of these brilliant and audacious actions—the
doughty, ubiquitous and presumptuous Paul, was himself an Englishman, not having the plea even of being
an American Colonist ; but it is to be observed that it
was a time of exceptional difficulty and misfortune in

Great Britain. Our struggle with America had been unsuccessful, and disaster had overtaken our arms there. Overjoyed at our humiliation, France and Holland took advantage of our weakness and declining prestige to supply the enemy with material for war, and France concluded a treaty of defensive alliance with America, the cementing of which convention had been the special object of Franklin and his brother commissioners' visit to the French Court.

But what was more grievous for England than even this, was the effete condition into which the navy had sunk. The incapable administration of the Admiralty, with Lord Sandwich as First Lord, had reached such a pitch that many officers of high professional rank refused to serve in any responsible post; ships were sent unseaworthy to sea, ill-equipped and worse provisioned; insubordination amongst officers and men was rife—in short, nothing could be more distressing to a lover of his country than to witness the disgrace that was settling down on that branch of the service that had done so much to make England respected and feared by other nations. Needless to say then that France was, no less than America, delighted beyond measure at the success of Paul's encounter with the *Drake;* it was then that, on the verge of war with England, she had publicly received the American plenipotentiaries. The French ambassador had left St James', the treaty was signed, and the French squadron was ready for sea.

Paul had captured many vessels and made many

prisoners, during his expeditions, and the commissioners, being very short of money, experienced
great difficulty in defraying the necessary expenses.
Much correspondence ensued upon this and upon
the subject of the command of the *Indien.* Incessant
quarrels and disputes with all in authority, whether
over or under him, must have made Paul quite as
great a trouble to his employers ashore as he was an
aid to them at sea. His importunity was endless.
Haughty, self-willed, and inordinately vain of his
prowess, he obviously believed that the American
cause was made for him, and not he for the cause;
and useful as he had proved himself in attacking, harassing and capturing British vessels, there can be no
doubt that in many ways he was a most embarrassing
and unmanageable instrument in their hands.

Franklin wrote him that the ship *Indien,* which had
been promised him by Congress, had been presented
to the King of France, and that he was to repair to
Versailles for further orders. In reply to this, Paul
answered haughtily that while thanking the commissioners for their communication, he begged to say that
he expected from Congress the first command of the
first squadron destined for an expedition, and that it
was as an admiral that he expected to sail, and proceeded at once to unfold his plans for the coming
campaign. These included the destruction of Whitehaven ; the seizure of the bank at Ayr, together with
the subsequent destruction of that town ; the burning
of Greenock and Port-Glasgow, together with the

shipping in the Clyde ; London was to be distressed by cutting off the supply of coal from Newcastle, and many towns on the coast of England and Scotland laid waste and burned. The destruction of the Baltic fleet was included in the programme. These projects were seriously propounded by Paul Jones.

Time went by, but still the wished-for appointment came not. At the desire, or with the approbation, of the King of France, M. de Sartine, the French Minister of Marine, had the intention of employing him in the French service. Day after day Paul pressed his services on both countries. Unable to control his impatience, he had applied to De Sartine for 'an unlimited command'; but France had many candidates for employment, and De Sartine must have regretted a promise he was unable to fulfil, at all events with the rapidity expected by this impatient and undisciplined young candidate. Promises, however, came thick from both Franklin and De Sartine; and at last, after ceaseless importunities, in the month of September 1779 he once more journeyed to Versailles, and was rewarded by the minister purchasing for him a frigate called the *Duc de Duras*.

He obtained leave to change her name to the *Bon Homme Richard*, observing that his success was an illustration of the truth of the saying of that character of Franklins imagination, ' Qui veut va, qui ne veut pas—envoie.' The *Alliance*, a new American frigate, to the command of which a Frenchman named Landais had been nominated, was to be one of a force

to be placed under Paul's orders.   This force consisted
of the *Pallas* the *Vengeance*, and the *Cerf*, with two
privateers, the *Monsieur* and the *Grandville*, all well
equipped and manned.   It was originally intended
that Lafayette, with 700 soldiers, was to be on board.
Well acquainted with Paul's imperious and overbearing temper, Franklin wrote and besought him to avoid
all misunderstandings with his companions in arms.
The squadron, he assured him, was to be entirely
under his command ; but Lafayette, being a major-
general, was entitled to a step in rank, and he must be
supreme over the land-forces.

Paul's reply was couched in terms of high-toned
chivalry.   'Where men of fine feelings are concerned,'
he said, 'there is seldom any misunderstanding.
Your noble-minded instructions would make a coward
brave.'

Early in September 1779, then, they sailed.   For
some reason or other, however, Lafayette and his
soldiers did not accompany them.   The squadron
beat about the coast of Scotland till the 13th, by
which time, and in consequence of some quarrel or
misunderstanding, the *Alliance*, together with the *Cerf*
and one privateer, had chosen to separate herself from
her fellows ; indeed, Paul seems to have been quite
unable to enforce the obedience that was his due.
Nothing can illustrate the unformed and, consequently, undisciplined condition of this incipient
navy better than the fact that the commodore was not
endowed with sufficient power to make such conduct

next to impossible.   It was at this time that he determined to make an effort to carry out his design of
destroying Leith.

The squadron sailed up the Firth of Forth, and
created a perfect panic, the coasts being entirely undefended, and the stories of his attack on Whitehaven
and his raid on St Mary's Isle having reached these
parts, probably in a greatly exaggerated form.   The
country was filled with alarm, and the peaceful
inhabitants of the towns and villages by the shore
were terrified and paralysed.   Pausing in Leith Roads,
he wrote a letter to the Provost of Leith, calling upon
him to pay the sum of £200,000, those being the
terms upon which he would consent to spare the
town; observing, that he should consider this as their
contribution towards the reimbursement owed by
Britain to the much-injured inhabitants of the United
States.   This document, which I believe still exists,
contains, however, the subjoined not wholly unimport-
ant postscript, written in his own hand: '*N.B.*—
The sudden and violent storm which arose in the
moment when the squadron was abreast of Keith
Island, which forms the entrance to the Road of Leith,
rendered impracticable the foregoing project.'

The 17th September, the day he approached Leith,
was on a Sunday.   Crowds from the towns and
villages flocked to the beach to gaze at the three ships
(for Landais and the *Alliance*, and the other two
before mentioned, had temporarily abandoned the
little fleet) which were causing so much excitement

and agitation. At one time the *Bon Homme Richard* was within a mile of the town of Kirkcaldy, and the alarm there was general. Divine service was being conducted in the kirk when the approach of the vessels was whispered amongst the congregation, who, followed by their minister, the Rev. Mr Shirra, hastened to the shore.

The interrupted prayer was resumed by the sea— a picturesque incident in this curious scene—when the earnest petition that the schemes of the 'piratical invader' should be defeated were, in the words of a member of the congregation, instantly answered: 'for even as he prayed the clouds gathered, the sky darkened, and this was shortly followed by a violent gale from the west,' which stopped all Paul's plans. * The conclusion of this abortive undertaking may be given in his own words :—

'We continued working to windward of the Firth,' he says, 'without being able to reach the Road of Leith till the morning of the 17th, when, being almost within cannon-shot of the town, and having everything in readiness for a descent, a very severe gale came on, and being directly contrary, obliged us to bear away, after having in vain for some time endeavoured to withstand its violence. The gale was so severe that

* An addition to this story appears in a number of *Blackwood's Magazine*, to the effect that when Mr Shirra seeing, with the experienced eye of a dweller on the east coast, that the sky and sea boded a change of wind,—'Weel dune, Lord !' said he, approvingly ; .'gie us anither puff.'

one of the prizes taken on the 14th sunk to the bottom, the crew being with difficulty saved.

'As the clamour had by this time reached Leith, by means of a cutter that had watched our motions that morning, and as the wind continued contrary, I thought it impossible to pursue the enterprise with a good prospect of success, especially as Edinburgh, where there is always a number of troops, is only a mile distant from Leith.   Therefore I gave up the project.'

Thus Paul rather naively acknowledges that he warred by preference against undefended towns, though, to do him justice, discretion was not the portion of valour that he most affected.

Emerging, then, from the Firth of Forth, he coasted southwards till he arrived off Scarborough, where he lay in wait watching for the merchant fleet that he knew was expected from the Baltic under the convoy of H.M.S. *Serapis*, Captain Pearson, and the *Countess of Scarborough* hired armed ship, Captain Piercy.   These two carried 64 guns and 380 men, protecting a fleet of which the cargo was valued at £600,000.   Paul Jones' squadron consisted of four ships, 126 guns, and 1100 men.

In the afternoon of September 23d (1779) he descried the fleet, with their escort, advancing north-east. He at once hoisted the signal for a general chase, whereupon the two English frigates stood out from land in battle array, while the merchantmen, crowding all sail, succeeded in taking refuge under the lee of the

guns of Scarborough Castle ; and Pearson, making all
the sail he could, managed to get between the enemy
and the merchant fleet. Signalling the latter to make
the best of their way, he brought the *Serapis* to, to
allow the *Countess of Scarborough* to come up, and
cleared his ship for action. Night was coming on
when the two ships, the *Serapis* and the *Bon Homme
Richard*, neared one another, and in a short time lay
black upon sea and land ; but presently a streak of
gold appeared upon the horizon, and the harvest
moon, slowly climbing the sky, lent her aureate light
to the actors of the bloody drama. So near to land
was the scene of action, that it was watched by
thousands of spectators with breathless and agonised
interest.

Neither vessel can have been said to have begun
the battle, for each fired a broadside simultaneously.
The two ships, after some fierce fighting, became entangled in each other's masts and sails. 'The
enemy's mizzen shrouds,' says Pearson, 'took the
Serapis' jib-boom, which hung him (the enemy) up
till at last it gave way, and the ships dropped alongside one another head and stern, while the muzzles of
the guns touched one another.'

At this juncture some old 18-pounders of the *Bon
Homme Richard* exploded, killing and wounding
several of Paul's crew. The flow of blood on board
the two ships but increased the fierceness of the fight,
and from deck to deck of the entangled vessels the
combatants rushed to and fro like demons, smeared

with blood and gunpowder, and fighting with cutlass, pike, and pistol. The *Bon Homme Richard* was struck by many heavy shots below water, and seemed in imminent danger of sinking. Paul, who is described as dressed in a short jacket and long trousers, his pistols slung in a belt round his middle, shot seven of his men for deserting their quarters, and he is said to have shot also at his nephew's legs, as he thought him '*a little dastardly.*' That this comparatively gentle act of expostulation took so mitigated a form must, we suppose, be ascribed to the tender ties of consanguinity. We are, unfortunately, uninformed as to the ultimate results to the young man, who but for his relationship would probably have shared the fate of the other seven.

The bowsprit of the *Serapis* coming athwart the poop of the *Bon Homme Richard*, Paul with a hawser made the two ships fast together. 'If my ship sinks, by —— she shall not sink alone,' he said. He was omnipresent, now directing the gunners, now urging the musketeers in the tops, everywhere in the thickest of the fight. Pearson, thus locked with the enemy, did terrific work with his guns on the under part of the *Bon Homme Richard*, while his own decks were literally swept by the musket-shot and hand-grenades that were fired and thrown with murderous effect by the enemy. Ten times was the *Serapis* on fire by the action of these combustibles, and she suffered considerably by the necessity of the crew having to extinguish the flames, a result that was effected with

great difficulty. The *Alliance,* which had now rejoined the squadron, sailed round and round the
Serapis, plying her with shot, and killing everyone
on deck. At nine an accident set fire to a cartridge
on board the *Serapis,* and the flame running from
cartridge to cartridge all the way aft, blew up all
the officers and men abaft the mainmast, thus rendering all the guns useless for the remainder of
the fight.

Exhausted with his almost superhuman exertions,
Paul sat down on the hencoop of his vessel, panting,
sinking, almost spent. At this moment his carpenter, wounded and half mad with excitement and
terror, called out that the *Bon Homme Richard* was
sinking.

A gunner, catching the infection, ran to pull down
the American colours, but a round-shot had done the
work long before.

'Quarter! for God's sake, quarter!' shouted the
gunner. Pearson, but a few feet distant, rose to the
sound.

'Do you cry for quarter?' he exclaimed.

'I have not yet BEGUN to fight,' responded Paul,
and with an oath he sprang from his short repose.

'Strike!' Pearson answered. 'Strike, or I will sink
you!' But the victory was not to Pearson, and the
conflict was resumed with greater desperation than
ever. At 10.30 the *Bon Homme Richard* was pour-
ing broadsides into the *Serapis,* without any possibility
of reply. Further resistance was useless. The end

had come. The English colours were struck, and the
mainmast at the same instant went by the board.

Rendering up his sword with the bitter remark that
Paul had fought with a halter round his neck, Pearson,
together with his lieutenant, was escorted on board
the *Bon Homme Richard*, where, in addition to the
crew, were 300 prisoners, captured by Paul during his
cruise, many of whom had rendered important service
during the battle in extinguishing fires. Pearson describes the ship as being in the utmost distress, her guns
dismounted, on fire in two places, with seven feet of
water in her hold. Nor did she long survive the desperate encounter; for the next day she sank from
injuries she had received—sank with many of the
wounded, unrescued by her inhuman commander, who,
together with his crew and some of his prisoners, went
over to the *Serapis*. The loss on board this ship was
not accurately ascertained. Pearson estimated it at
49 killed and 68 wounded, out of a crew of 170 men.

The carnage on board the *Bon Homme Richard* was
almost unprecedented. At the end of the engagement
the deck was literally streaming with the blood of
three-fourths of the whole crew, who were killed and
wounded in the action. The *Countess of Scarborough*
had engaged the *Pallas*, 32 guns, while the other
conflict was proceeding.

The weather was very boisterous, and Paul's
squadron and prizes drove about the North Sea
for some days, until the 3d October, when they
came to anchor in the Texel. The engagement was

one of the most desperate and obstinately contested in the records of naval warfare.

Pearson and Piercy were transferred, by exchange of prisoners, to London, where they were received by the king with marks of great favour. The former was knighted by his Majesty, and the Royal Exchange Assurance Company, who had £20,000 underwritten on the ships that were under their convoy, and that had been rescued at such a cost, presented each of those officers with a piece of plate in token of gratitude, and to show their appreciation of their gallantry.

Pearson became eventually Governor of Greenwich Hospital, and died there at an advanced age.

The news of this disaster to the British ships rang through Great Britain. Paul Jones' name was in every mouth; his deeds, his prowess, his daring, the universal theme. Franklin wrote at once, congratulating him in the most flattering terms, and assuring him that the conduct of Landais, of whom Paul had written in the most indignant and bitter terms—accusing him of dastardly and treasonable actions—should be punished, and that he should be ordered to render himself up at once to give an account of himself to the commissioners.

But his arrival in the Texel and at Amsterdam was a by no means welcome incident to the Court of Holland, and was fraught with much annoyance to himself and all concerned.

Franklin had ordered him, when he had finished his cruise, to take shelter there, possibly with a view to hustling the Dutch out of their political neutrality. The United States, supported by France, Spain, and Holland, would, he believed, prove more than a match for Great Britain in her present demoralised condition. And now began a sharp altercation between the English ambassador Sir Joseph Yorke, and the Dutch Government. The latter had already committed several virtual infractions of the treaty of alliance with England, by supplying both America and France with maritime and warlike stores ; but the outward and visible sign of their disloyalty, displaying itself in the unopposed arrival in the Dutch waters of the triumphant American commodore, red-handed from the fight—exulting in his complete and brilliant victory, with his magnificent trophies, the two English frigates in his wake—was one step beyond what could be endured by Great Britain.

Sir Joseph Yorke presented a memorial couched in the most peremptory terms, requiring that the English ships ' taken by one Paul Jones, a subject of the King of Great Britain, who, according to treaties and the laws of war, falls under the class of rebels and pirates,' should be detained in the Texel.

The Dutch knew not how to extricate themselves from this most perplexing dilemma. They were not yet prepared for war with England, but they were very unwilling to offend France and America ; so they tried to evade it by declaring that they gave shelter to all ships whatsoever in stress of weather, but compelled armed ships with their prizes to put to sea as soon as possible. This was entirely unsatisfactory. To protect Paul was to recognise the independence of America, and so far as that they dare not go. Sir Joseph, however, gave them no peace; in their turn they assailed the French ambassador, while this last retaliated on Paul, who was placed literally between the devil and the deep sea, for there were English ships at the entrance of the Texel lying in wait for him at his exit, while light squadrons cruised about to prevent his giving them the slip and gaining any French or Spanish harbour should he contrive to avoid them.

The controversy went on till December. At last the French ambassador bethought himself of a plan. He persuaded Franklin to consent that the captured frigates should be placed under the French flag, and that Paul should be removed to the *Alliance*, the only American ship in commission there, which, as Landais had been ordered to Paris, had no commander, and after a long altercation with him, Paul was compelled to yield and quit the *Serapis*—at once the theatre and manifestation of his glory—and translate himself on board the *Alliance;* so the French squadron sailed gaily away, leaving Paul smarting with indignation under the insulting epithets bestowed upon him by Sir J. Yorke, and a prey to bitter and humiliating reflections. He had been received at Amsterdam on his arrival with the wildest enthusiasm by the populace. Crowds followed and huzzaed him. The Amsterdam press—strongly in sympathy with

America—praised him in the most fulsome terms. He was spoken of as the brave, the intrepid, the generous. When he appeared on 'Change on 14th October, all business was temporarily suspended to gaze at and follow him. He was attired in a blue frock-coat, metal buttons, and white cloth waistcoat and breeches, and carried a broadsword under his arm. Quiting 'Change, the crowd followed him to his lodging, cheering him all the way home.

Several of his seamen deserted him in the Texel, but some of the Dutch people betrayed them. They were retaken, and cruelly maltreated by their commander, who put them in irons, reduced their allowance of food, and severely flogged them. One midshipman was so harshly treated that his life was despaired of. He was styled 'the terror of the English.' While at Amsterdam he put into American agents' hands bills to the amount of 80,000 guineas, for them to procure payment—and he had more in his possession. A letter describes him as of middle height, thin and strongly built, strong-featured, usually wearing a *roquelaure* over his uniform, with a large cape edged with gold lace. 'He has enjoyed himself on land,' it says, 'without showing the least compassion to his wounded crew or his prisoners; but some surgeons were sent on board, it not being permitted in neutral ports to land the wounded. There is one De Nau, a merchant, who expects to be agent for the Americans. He has been very polite to Paul Jones, who lives in his house. He sent a vessel to this self-styled admiral in the Texel, loaded with provisions.'

After the departure of the French fleet, Paul's position became still more unpleasant; and, having a good deal of time upon his hands, he drew up a 'Memorial' to the King of France, setting forth his merits and his services; and he also indited the following insulting and flippant letter to Lord Sandwich, which, as far as I know, has not been printed in any of his memoirs :—

'*October* 9, 1779.

'MY LORD,—I should think myself the most ungrateful of men living, were I not to take the earliest opportunity of expressing the great obligations I am under to your lordship in permitting me for so long a time to seize, plunder, and carry off the vessels of the merchants in the British and Irish seas; and I am perfectly sensible, my lord, I should not have done so but by your lordship's kind permission. It was a favour, my lord, which much exceeded my warmest expectations, and as it has made my fortune and raised my reputation as a gallant seaman, I most heartily thank your lordship for it. At the first I was something puzzled to account for your lordship's favour to me; but, upon a little consideration I became sensible that a similarity of principles, lives, and circumstances, generally begets a mutual affection between men, and there appears to be a very strong and striking likeness between your lordship's principles, life, and circumstances, when compared with my own. To be like so great a man as your lordship flatters my vanity much, and therefore you will excuse me, my lord, if I mention some of the features of our similarity.

'Your lordship and I do both of us heartily despise all the musty rules of religion; your lordship and I do both agree that speaking truth is vulgar and disgraceful; your lordship and I think it an honour to procure riches by any means whatsoever. You and I, my lord, have both of us plundered the British nation, and are therefore become opulent; you and I, my lord, are both of us hated and dreaded by the people of England, and as our principles, lives, and circumstances are so very similar, it is great odds that our deaths will be the same. Having thus indulged my vanity by showing the great likeness between your lordship and myself, which was doubtless the cause of your permitting me to plunder the merchants so long in your seas, I think it my duty to inform your lordship that I am now got safe into port to refit and victual my fleet, where I shall be (*sic*) retained for some time, but flatter myself with the hopes of paying your lordship another visit in the British seas before the winter is over, when I make no doubt your lordship will again repeat the same favour to a man who is so perfectly like yourself as

'PAUL JONES.'

To Paul's intense mortification and indignation, a

commission was now tendered to him by France of a description that roused his most indignant remonstrances. He received the offer of a letter of marque. Penetrated as he was with a sense of his own genius, importance, and dignity, it can be imagined how he received this proof of the disesteem with which he was regarded by France. His resentment knew no bounds, and resulted in a letter addressed to the French ambassador at the Hague—the Duc de Vauguyon—through whose medium the offer had been made, which is couched in a more dignified tone than any other composition of his that is extant.

There were men, he said, who might feel honoured at the offer of such a commission; but the navy of America knew no superior in rank to himself, and he could accept no appointment of equal, or even superior, rank to that he bore, unless authorised by Congress. It was matter of astonishment to him, he added, that the Court should suppose him capable of disgracing his present commission in such a way.

This letter drew from the ambassador some soothing words, which had more or less the desired effect; but Paul quitted the Texel, disappointed, mortified and humiliated. Eluding the vigilance of those on watch for him, he gained L'Orient, having passed, unrecognised and unsuspected, through the Straits of Dover in full view of a portion of the British fleet, then lying in the Downs. Next day he ran the *Alliance* past the Isle of Wight, in view of the enemy's fleet at Spithead, and in two more days got safe through the Channel and with little delay arrived at Groix on the 10th February. The middle of April (1780) found Paul under orders to proceed to America ; but, with the defiant independence which characterised him, he went to Versailles, he asserted, to obtain the prize-money for his crew. The American commodore—the conqueror of the English—insulted at Amsterdam by the offer of a letter of marque from the French ambassador was received in Paris with open arms, and speedily became the lion of the day—*fêté* and caressed by the highest of the land.

He was welcomed at Court with the utmost graciousness by the King and Queen. The former presented him with a golden sword, with the following legend engraved upon it :—' Vindicati maris Ludovicus XVI. remunerator strenuo vindici.' The Military Order of Merit was bestowed upon him, and he received an official letter from M. de Sartine expressive of the highest esteem and approbation. Intensely delighted with his reception and success in society, Paul forgot the insult of the letter of marque, and fairly revelled in the atmosphere of flattery which surrounded him. ' I received,' he says, ' the most flattering applause and public approbation wherever I appeared. Both the great and the learned sought my acquaintance in private life, and honoured me with particular marks of friendship. At Court I was always received with a kindness which could only have arisen from a fixed esteem.'

Confident of success, he solicited and obtained the

Ariel frigate to accompany the *Alliance* to America, with stores for Washington's army ; and, in high spirits, he quitted Versailles and returned to L'Orient.

During his absence, the *Alliance* had broken out in mutinous revolt. The delay of the payment of the prize-money and non-payment of seamen's arrears had caused serious discontent amongst the crew. Landais, following Paul's example, had failed to obey official orders to return to America ; and he had determined to reassume the command of the *Alliance*, which he had been compelled to forego. Franklin seems from some cause or other to have been incapable of insisting, and only remonstrated. Paul had accused Landais and the crew of the *Alliance*, of firing into the *Bon Homme Richard* during the affair with the *Serapis*, and the crew were naturally furious with their traducer, and refused to serve under him. Officers and men unanimously resolved to defend Landais, should Paul, as he threatened, attempt to seize him ; and they made every preparation to repel force by force. Paul demanded of the authorities 400 men to quell the revolted crew ; but taking advantage of the darkness of night, Landais caused himself to be towed to Port Louis—a most daring enterprise—and set sail at once for America.

Thus foiled Paul became temporarily as great a nuisance to the French Government as he had been in former days to the American. The *Ariel* was laden with military stores, which it was of the highest import- ance should be at once transported to America ; but still he dallied, in hopes of extracting more ships from France to add to the importance of his command. At last he set sail, but was the very next day overtaken by so violent a gale, that he was compelled to put back to refit and make good the injuries he had sustained. Reckless as to expenditure, and regardless of Franklin's earnest exhortations to be more careful on this point, he proceeded to the most lavish outlays on the ship. No remonstrance had the smallest effect on this disobedient commander; and after many weeks' procrastination, he could find no further excuses, and sailed in earnest, arriving at Philadelphia in February 1781.

An official inquiry as to the cause of the retarded delivery of the stores was instituted on his arrival, but he satisfied his inquisitors, and the Admiralty delivered a most flattering report of his services, concluding by recommending some distinguished mark of approbation from the United States in Congress assembled; and he received their solemn thanks for his services. Washington wrote him in approving terms, and at this moment there seems to have been nothing wanting to fill his measure of gratification.

To complete his triumph, Congress resolved 'that a gold medal should be struck and presented to Chevalier J. Paul Jones, in commemoration of the valour and brilliant services of that officer while in command of a squadron of French and American ships, under the flag and commission of the States of America.'

Peace being soon after declared, Paul solicited an appointment in Europe as prize-agent, for there were

still large sums due to his crews. With his usual
flourish, he called this 'an embassy,' and it proved a
vexatious and troublesome undertaking. For several
years he lived in Paris, where he extended his former
social connections, and took a prominent part in
fashionable society. He repeatedly had his portrait
painted and his bust executed, giving these away
amongst his acquaintances; he also handed about the
journal of his campaigns, receiving—and keeping—all
the letters of adulation with which it was acknowledged.

An adjustment of the prize-money was arranged in
1787, and Paul returned to America. Congress, whose
attitude towards Paul bears some resemblance to that
of the judge in Scripture towards the importunate
widow, received at this time an application from him
to give him a letter of recommendation to the French
king for employment. In this he called their attention to all his services and successes under the American flag, alluding to the gold-hilted sword as 'an
honour which his Majesty had never conferred on any
other officer,' and making large personal pecuniary
claims. The claims were allowed; and thus Paul—a
living example of the wisdom and astuteness of the
policy of self-esteem and importunity—triumphant
over his enemies, exulting in his honours sailed away
from the land of his adoption in search of a fresh
field for his genius and his sword.

Arrived in Paris, Mr Jefferson, the American envoy
there, informed him that some correspondence had

passed between himself and M. de Simolin, the
Russian ambassador, on the subject of Paul serving
the Russians. Disaster had fallen on the imperial
fleet the preceding autumn, and it had been suggested
that Paul's experience and talents might be of much
service. It is difficult to form an opinion as to
whether the proposal really emanated from Russia,
or whether Paul, in some previous correspondence of
his own, had paved the way for his path into the
service of the Empress Catherine II. In any case
he was beyond measure dazzled and delighted at the
dawning possibilities of further laurels thus opened
up, and deferring the delivery of the letter to the
French king, set out immediately for Copenhagen.
He was furnished with letters to the French ambassador, and gives a most flowery and elaborate account of his intercourse with that functionary, and
of his reception by the Danish king and queen.

Negotiations with the Russian ambassador were
at once commenced, and a commission in the Russian
navy of captain-commandant, with a command in
the Black Sea, under the orders of Prince Potemkin,
was offered to him. Paul, however, demurred. He
requested, and indeed insisted, on the grade of rear-
admiral being accorded to him ; but difficulties being
made, he resolved to seek an interview with the
Empress, and with the energy and determination
that characterised all his actions, he left Copenhagen
for St Petersburg. His journey was performed under
the most difficult and trying circumstances. Arrived

at Stockholm, he proceeded to Gravöe, where the
ice presented an insuperable obstacle to his crossing
the Gulf of Bothnia. He made several unsuccessful
efforts to get to Finland by the islands, but being
baffled, he left Gravöe early one morning, in an un-
decked boat, 30 feet long, followed by another half
that size. This last was for dragging over the ice
and passing from one piece of ice to another to gain
the coast of Finland. All day they kept along the
coast of Sweden, experiencing great difficulty in passing between the ice and the shore. Towards night,
being still nearly opposite Stockholm, he forced the
unwilling boatmen by threats, to enter the Baltic,
and steer for Finland. They ran near the coast, and
the wind being fair all day, they hoped to land the
following, but the ice did not permit them to approach
the shore. It was impossible to regain the Swedish
side, the wind increased in force, and turned contrary,
so they were compelled to stand for the Gulf of Finland. They lost the small boat; but the men saved
themselves, and entered the larger one, which with
difficulty escaped the same fate, and at the end of
four days' hardships they landed at Revel. Paying
his men for their services, Paul arrived, four days later
—on the 23d April 1788—at St Petersburg. Catherine received him graciously, the coveted rank was
accorded, and on the 7th May he left the Russian
capital, carrying with him a letter from her Imperial
Majesty to the Prince-Marshal Potemkin, at St
Elizabeth's, where he arrived on the 19th. Paul was

probably unaware of the character of the despot into
whose iron grip he was about to be resigned.   Potemkin was one of the most extraordinary men of the
time, and played a conspicuous and important part in
the history of the Russia of the eighteenth century.
An inconceivable mixture of barbarism and civilisation, pomp and satiety, brilliancy and vandalism, devotion to the Empress and of iron self-will, no design
was too preposterous, no action too extravagant for
him to accomplish.   He suffered no hindrance to, or
interference with, his arbitrary will, and thus it is
hardly matter for surprise that Paul should be in a
sense unequal to the position assigned to him.

He was at once despatched to assume the command of
a portion of the naval force stationed in the Liman, to
act against the Turks who were defending Oczakow.
It would be impossible and tedious to follow him
through this campaign, which appears to have been,
as far as he was concerned, one uninterrupted series
of disputes.   Failures in enterprises were the logical
results.   Paul charged the Prince of Nassau, who was
associated with him in his command, with incapacity,
cowardice, falsehood—in a word, with every crime and
folly that could disgrace an officer.   Faults there
were, doubtless, on both sides, but Paul's insufferable
arrogance and insolence made matters intolerable to
all who had dealings with him.   He attempted to
assume both commands, and although he may have
been the abler man of the two, the fact could hardly
be acted upon, even had it been satisfactorily demon-

strated. Nor was it reasonable to expect that the Prince would quietly permit Paul to reduce him to a cipher. Paul's refusal to obey orders was the cause of many mishaps; and although his tactics and knowledge of war may have exceeded those of his equals, yet his insubordination gave right to the other side. The flotilla of which the Prince of Nassau was in command got all the credit of some actions to which Paul laid claim. Catherine had sent out orders, medals, and some gold-hilted swords to be distributed at Potemkin's pleasure to those who had taken part in the different actions; but to his mortification Paul only received the Order of St Anne, while the officers of his squadron were passed over. The Prince of Nassau received an estate, a diamond-hilted sword, and the Order of St George, second class. There were five orders of knighthood in Russia: three instituted by Peter the Great, and two —those of St George and St Vladimir—by Catherine II. The Order of St Anne was a Holstein and not a Russian order. The Empress never conferred it herself. She left it to the Grand-Duke Paul, as Duke of Holstein, and from him Paul received it. It was, of course, less valued than those of her own institution bestowed by herself, hence Paul's mortification.

At this time Potemkin issued an order, couched in language that so offended Paul, that he lost all command of himself, and replied in such terms that he was at once recalled, and was superseded by Admiral

Morduruoff, who assumed the command of Paul's squadron and the Prince of Nassau's flotilla. Paul was, however, invited to headquarters to take leave, and he appealed to Potemkin to reinstate him. Potemkin refused, and he was ordered to St Petersburg. It was hinted to him, however, that he might receive the command of the fleet in the North Sea. He journeyed to the Russian capital, and obtained an audience of the Empress. It is asserted that the English officers who were serving in the North Sea with the Russian fleet refused to fight if Paul were appointed. Whether or no this is true, it is, at anyrate, a fact that Paul received neither that nor any other command from the Empress. He fell into disgrace, and was accused of scandalous conduct towards a young girl: his friends indignantly denied the truth of the statement, and asserted that the story was got up by his enemies.

Hitherto Catherine had countenanced him so far that she permitted him to present himself before her, but after this she commanded him to appear in her presence no more. He wrote an explanation and justification of his conduct, and so far exculpated himself as to be again permitted to go to Court, but it was merely for the ceremony of taking leave of the Empress, and he was virtually dismissed from Russia. From St Petersburg he went for a short time to Warsaw, where he became intimate with the Polish patriot Kosciusko. Sweden was at this time in the heat of war with Russia, and Paul secretly intrigued to take service under Gustavus III., his project being eagerly supported by Kosciusko. He was at the same moment, it may be added, making efforts to obtain pardon from Russia and employment in her navy, so that his desire to fight for Sweden was looked upon by him only as a *pis aller*. His efforts failing, he returned to Amsterdam, and there remained till the spring of the following year, 1790, when he went for a short time to England, and on landing at Harwich was threatened with the vengeance of the populace. He escaped from their fury and got to London, and after remaining there a short time he went to Paris. His health was broken, and he became subject to sudden and severe attacks of indisposition, but he still clung to the hope of serving Russia. He addressed the Empress, he wrote to Potemkin. His letter to the latter is full of invective against his 'enemies,' of self-praise, of assertions that any successes of the campaign of the Liman were due to him and to him alone. He requests that the Order of St George shall be accorded to him ; he enumerates his merits and his claims.

Whether Potemkin replied to this appeal or not we are not aware. We do not think that he did ; but Catherine caused a letter to be written, telling him that there were prospects of a speedy peace ; but should her prognostications not be verified, she would let Paul Jones know her intentions regarding him.

Here Paul's active career ended ; here terminated alike his hopes and his health. There is little doubt that disappointment and mortification contributed

to hasten his end. He died in Paris in July 1792,
having suffered shortly before from an acute attack
of jaundice, which was followed by dropsy.

The American ambassador did not claim his remains, nor did the United States pay any honours to
the dust of one from whom they had derived so much
glory. The National Assembly of France sent a depu-
tation to attend his funeral, and a fulsome oration was
made at his grave. He was buried in Pere la Chaise.

Of his personal appearance, save that he was short
and thick-set with bushy eyebrows and swarthy complexion, there is not much to learn, and I have been
unable to find any print of him, although I believe
some exist.* A bold and skilful seaman, fertile in
expedients, of iron will and dauntless valour, there is
ample evidence of his violent and implacable temper
and of his jealous and tyrannical disposition. He was
hated by both officers and men, and during his whole
life he does not appear to have formed a single friendship. His determination and indifference as to the
means by which he compassed his ends, were his
chief characteristics, together with a certain brutal in-
flexibility which was discovered early in life by the
murder of Mungo Maxwell.

In all the accounts of his adventures and his battles,
we never hear of his being overcome by any softness
of feeling, or melted to pity by any suffering. We
hear of no friendship formed, no generous deed done.

* Since the first publication of this sketch in *Blackwood's Magazine*,
a gentleman in America kindly sent me an interesting portrait of him.

Jealous of all who were associated with him in his profession, he invariably and revengefully quarrelled with them, and endeavoured to deny them any praise or merit in any undertaking in which he took part.

Singularly capable, with great powers of endurance, his powerful will and unscrupulous temper swept all obstacles from his path, and made him a leader of men. He was a living contradiction of the commonly received belief that all brave men are generous-minded ones, and all bullies cowards. He embraced the cause of America because it suited his ambition to do so ; but when he saw the chance of distinguishing himself in the Russian service, he quickly abandoned the democratic principles that he had so loudly applauded, and proclaimed his devotion to the imperial cause.

In spite of all his conciliatory and commendatory letters to Paul, Franklin was too keen a judge of human nature not to discover what manner of man he was ; but Paul possessed too many of the qualities needed in such a struggle as that in which America was engaged, for Franklin to be fastidious. His object was to deliver his country, and when this incisive and efficient instrument was placed in his hands he made use of it, but found it was not cast out of unalloyed metal. Intensely vain, Paul's boastfulness and swagger must have been, together with his want of truth, a sore trial, as well as an obstruction and an offence, to the upright Franklin's dealings and feelings.

We are so accustomed to see chivalry and generosity

go hand in hand with courage, that we are amazed when we see so much that is contemptible and mean united in the person of anyone so distinguished for his valour and achievements.

He has left but a very slight mark in history; his deeds are not remembered, his prowess is forgotten, his name has nearly died out.

He had great qualities and extraordinary strength of will : and to such as are acquainted with the history of that perturbed period, there may perhaps occur a little thrill of gratification at the reflection that America, our rebellious and victorious offspring, owed her first naval triumph to an Englishman, even though that Englishman was a renegade and a time-server.

LORD GEORGE GORDON AND THE
RIOTS OF 1780

LORD GEORGE GORDON AND
THE RIOTS OF 1780

LORD GEORGE GORDON, the subject of this sketch, was born in 1752. He was the second son of Cosmo, third Duke of Gordon, his mother being a daughter of William, second Earl of Aberdeen—himself the representative of a branch of the distinguished House of Gordon. The Duke died before the birth of his youngest son, and eventually his widow married a gentleman of the name of Morris.

All through the seventeenth century the Head of the Gordon family and his descendants were staunch upholders of the Roman Catholic faith, but the marriage of Alexander, second Duke, with Henrietta Mordaunt, a daughter of Charles, Earl of Peterborough, the General who attached himself to the Prince of Orange in those troublous times, worked a change in the thoughts and feelings of her husband's lineage, and it has been asserted that the Duchess of Gordon

was rewarded by a pension of £1000 a year for her
achievement in converting that noble House from the
errors of Popery.

Lord George Gordon entered the Navy when a boy,
and after serving in America and the West Indies in
due time became a lieutenant. Returning home he
conceived the project of representing Inverness-shire in
Parliament, and of ousting Fraser of Lovat, the sitting
member—a much rarer and bolder undertaking in
those days than now. Fraser was a potentate in his
own country, and it must have been as great a surprise as mortification to find that a mere boy had
superseded him and secured the seat, whose tenure he
regarded with as great a sense of ownership as he did
Beauly Castle. Lord George at this time is described
as being possessed of good looks and a winning address, and to have had the art of making himself
popular with all classes. He spoke Gaelic, was courteous and agreeable, and gave on the occasion of his
successful election an magnificent ball at Inverness,
hiring a ship to bring thither from the Isle of Sky
fifteen young ladies—all of the family of M'Leod—all
beautiful, and the pride and admiration of the High-
lands. It was not, however, to be endured that this
stripling should bear away the chieftain's honours
thus, and it was arranged between Lovat and the
Duke of Gordon that the latter should purchase for
his son an English borough. He was therefore duly
returned for Ludyershall at the election of 1774.

With a very inaccurate estimate of his own abilities,

Lord George entered Parliament with the avowed intention of supporting Lord North's Ministry, then in power. Lord Sandwich was First Lord of the Admirality, and he before long applied to that Minister for his naval promotion. The request was altogether unreasonable. He had distinguished himself in no way, and had it been granted, he would have been placed over the heads of other far more deserving officers. Lord Sandwich very properly refused the application, and Lord George forthwith quitted the Ministerial benches and went over to the Opposition.

He was patronised by Fox and Burke, who desired to engage him to their side; and in 1776 he made his first notable speech, delivering an intemperate and passionate philippic against the Government, and asserting that they had endeavoured to bribe him from the Opposition by the offer of a sinecure of £1000 a year. If this were true, there can be no doubt that they put a far greater value on his support than it was worth; and if he really refused a bribe, it is possible that he resented that his magnanimity was not more appreciated, for before long he began to disunite himself from both parties of the State, proclaiming himself to be that voracious seeker after popularity, 'a friend of the people.'

He rapidly became a nuisance in the House of Commons, for of wit and wisdom—the only terms upon which any departure from the ordinary course of business can be tolerated there—he was destitute, and his eccentricity of dress and manner grew to such an excess that he was looked upon as partially insane. He insulted the Ministry, badgered the Opposition, interrupted the course of business,* continually bringing in matters concerning religion and the dangers of Popery, in a manner wholly irrelevant to the matters under discussion, and he divided the House on questions wherein he stood alone, and was, in short, not only singular, but offensive and irrepressible.

At one time he took up the Irish question, and feeling no doubts that he could solve all difficulties, reduced his views to a pamphlet, with which he proceeded to Buckingham House, demanded, and obtained, an audience of the King, 'and began,' says Horace Walpole, 'to read it incontinently' to him. His Majesty listened with courteous attention to the apparently interminable argument, but at length the day began to decline so rapidly that it was difficult to distinguish the print. Eagerly availing himself of the heaven-sent means of escape, George III. begged that he might be excused the rest. Nothing daunted, however, by the signs of the King's fatigue, Lord George extracted the royal word of honour that he would finish the pamphlet, and, having obtained this concession, at length took his departure.

To some enlightened and benevolent minds it seemed desirable about this time that certain penalties and disabilities suffered by the Roman Catholics since

* Then, as unfortunately now, in the power of any indifferent speaker.—*Ed.*

the time of William III. should be repealed. A Bill
'to prevent the further growth of Popery' had been
passed in that reign, some clauses of which were, as
Sir George Savile, who moved for leave to bring in
the Relief Act, said, entirely opposed to the principles
of Protestantism. Framed in the most moderate
spirit, only certain clauses were named for absolute repeal; and, at the end of a temperate and well-reasoned
speech, Sir George instanced, as an inducement to the
House, the loyal and peaceful behaviour of those who
had for so long suffered such intolerable persecution.
The clauses to which he objected were : the liability
of all Popish priests and Jesuits to perpetual imprison-
ment should they take upon themselves the education
of youth, or the keeping of schools in the realm, or
should they officiate in their places of worship; the
forfeiture of Popish heirs educated abroad and whose
estates devolved upon the next Protestant heir, powers
being given to the son or other nearest relative—being
a Protestant—to take possession of the father's or
other relation's estate, during the life of the real pro-
prietor; and the depriving of Papists from acquiring
any legal property by purchase.

Sir George Savile was a Whig, and a man respected by both parties; and his speech was so full
of good sense and feeling, so moderate and well considered, that the motion was carried without a dissen-
tient voice, and the Bill was passed. Many Roman
Catholics of all grades came forward to express their
gratitude for this gracious and benevolent act, and

R

with the most ardent professions of attachment to the
King and the Government; and the expected good
effects of the indulgence seemed in a fair way of being
realised. This Act, however, did not extend to Scotland; and no sooner did it become law in England
than the Roman Catholics there, naturally desirous of
partaking of the benefits of their co-religionists, sent
a petition to Parliament praying that they might be
included in the Relief Act. No sooner was this known
than the rumour was bruited about that the Legislature
contemplated granting their prayer, and the Scotch
people at once became exasperated at the prospect of
the victims being delivered from what they deemed
merited sufferings. Associations were formed, meetings convened, speeches made, pamphlets published,
and the whole of Scotland thrilled with rancorous
indignation.

It was resolved to send a counter petition to oppose
the Roman Catholics, and a form was promptly prepared, setting forth all the advantages that had accrued
to Christianity in general and Protestantism in particular by the persecutions and humiliations suffered
by their Popish brethren, and praying their rulers to
resist the threatened remission of their penalties.
One leaflet in particular appeared in Edinburgh which
stirred the people to their depths. It was as
follows :—

'MEN AND BRETHREN,—Whoever shall find this
letter, will take it as a warning to meet at Leith Wynd

on Wednesday next, to pull down that pillar of Popery lately erected there.

'(Signed)   A PROTESTANT.'

'*P.S.*—Please read this carefully, keep it clean, and drop it somewhere else—addressed to every Protestant into whose hands this shall come.—Jan. 1st, 1779.'

In Leith Wynd a Roman Catholic bishop resided, and it was, perhaps correctly, surmised that there existed under his roof a chapel.

What with angry resolutions, violent pamphlets and handbills, the population were worked up into such a state of exasperation, that on the 2d February, 1779, their fury exploded with irrepressible wrath. Nor did they confine their acts of vengeance to Roman Catholics alone. Protestants who were suspected of sympathising with the unpopular religion were marked as victims for their deeds of violence. The magistrates assembled, together with a regiment of fencibles, but they were powerless to restrain the mob, who destroyed the bishop's house, as well as those of many other suspects. Unable or afraid to take decided measures, the magistrates, to their disgrace, assured the people that no repeal of the penal laws against Papists should take place, and quiet was temporarily restored. Other Scottish towns, encouraged by the metropolitan success, took the same steps, with the same result ; and Lord Weymouth, the Home Secretary, wrote confirming the assurances given them by their Syndics. So much did the Roman Catholics suffer during this

agitated period from the hands of their Christian
Scottish brethren, that they deemed it prudent to
memorialise Parliament again—not for the relief
that had been won for their fellow-sufferers, but for
the immediate protection of their own lives and
properties.　Burke was their medium, and on the 18th
March he laid their petition before the House; and
it was on this occasion that Lord George made his
first appearance in the character of the Champion of
the Protestant privilege to persecute Papists. *

In August Lord George visited Edinburgh, and was
there received with the most extravagant expressions
of welcome and confidence.　Undeserved honours always turn the heads of the recipients, and Lord George
was no exception to this rule.　Flattered at the ova-
tion accorded to him, he, by his incendiary speeches
and appeals, fanned the smouldering fire of Scottish
anger, and on returning to London deliberately proceeded to sow the seeds of similar wrathful fanaticism
there.

The reception he had met with in Edinburgh induced the 'Protestant Association'—jealous of the
success with which Scotland had opposed the Relief
Act on their own behalf—to nominate him their
President, a post which he accepted in an evil moment
for all concerned.　This Association had been formed
in February, 1778, for the purpose of opposing the

---

* In the month of April the sum of £16co was awarded by arbitra-
tion to the Roman Catholics of Edinburgh, which sum was paid by
that city.　Nineteen rioters were apprehended, examined, and set at
liberty.

Act of Concessions, and contained a multitude of persons of all ranks and grades, but more especially of the lower. By sermons, placards, pamphlets, ballads and handbills they incessantly endeavoured to arouse popular indignation against the Roman Catholics. The lower classes were told that both King and Ministers were to be assassinated by the Pope's orders, and that 20,000 Jesuits were hidden in the caves of Surrey ready to blow up the banks and bed of the Thames, so as to drown out London and Westminster. They made an 'Appeal to the People of England,' stating that to 'tolerate Popery is to be instrumental in the perdition of immortal souls' . . . . 'Popery is not only High Treason against King and State, but against God' . . . . . 'The present Act has put the Sword in the Papists' hands, and England will be deluged with the blood of Martyrs.'

After a few skirmishes in the House, Lord George Gordon on the 5th May presented a petition from Plymouth for the repeal of Sir George Savile's Act, but little heed was paid to it.

Indignant at what he was pleased to condemn as weakness, Lord George called a meeting of the Protestant Association at Coachmakers' Hall, Foster Lane, on the 29th May, and in a fanatical and inflammatory speech asserted that alarming progress was being made in Popery, and the only way to stem the tide was by going in a firm, manly and resolute manner to the House of Commons and showing their

representatives that they were resolved to maintain
their religious freedom with their lives.   As for him,
he said, he was determined to throw in his part and
run all hazards with and for the people, and if they
proved themselves too lukewarm, and less than 20,000
of his fellow-citizens attended him on the appointed
day, he would refuse to present their petition.   A resolution was then passed that the whole body of the
Association should meet on the following Friday,
June 2d, in St George's-in-the-Fields, to accompany
Lord George to the House of Commons to present
the Protestant petition.   Many temperate men and
good Protestants no less desirous of the welfare of
their religion than the fanatics refused their support,
anticipating some of the dangers which resulted.

Lord George invited 'all true Protestants of Great
Britain' and 'all friends of civil and religious liberty'
to meet him to support the Protestant interest, and
exhorted all who had not already signed the petition
to attend at his house in Welbeck Street, where it lay
for 'further signatures.   The people, he added, were
all to be dressed in their best, and to be distinguished
by the wearing of a blue cockade.   He declared that
the King was a Papist at heart, and had violated the
Coronation Oath, and 'had placed himself in the
same predicament as James II. after his abdication.'

Lord George need have been under no apprehension lest the numbers stipulated by him as a condition
of his patronage should fall short, for by ten o'clock
on the morning of Friday, June 2d, an enormous

multitude had assembled at the appointed rendezvous.
All the shops in the neighbourhood were closed, for
the gathering together of such a throng of people was
in itself a sufficient cause of uneasiness in the breasts
of orderly and peaceable people ; and as the mob
arrived from every quarter, wearing the blue cockade,
and many bearing banners of the same colour inscribed
with mottoes inimical to Popery, the noise of this
enormous assemblage—estimated at from 60,000 to
100,000 people—is described as resembling the surg-
ing of the waves of the sea.   Every unit of the crowd
seemed labouring under the most intense excitement,
which found vent in various ways—some in singing
hymns, some in wildly shouting the words inscribed
on the banners they carried, whilst the mere fact of
such an assemblage of human beings congregated
together, added to the electric excitement with which
the very air seemed charged.   At twelve o'clock the
scouts, who were posted on the outskirts of the crowd
to give the first warning of Lord George's arrival,
announced his approach.   Descending from his coach
he passed amongst the people who were standing expectant, whilst many of them broke out into a chorus
to a hymn tune as he passed down the lines inspecting his vagabond battalions, who, under the guidance
and discipline of some of his selected followers had
been drilled into semi-military order.   Several bodies
under suitable commanders occupied different parts
of the field—each division formed by lines of nine
men abreast—all decked with blue cockades, and

the words 'No Popery' on their floating blue ribbons.

The Petition, which had grown to such enormous proportions that one man was unable to carry it, was lifted on to men's shoulders, and occupied a conspicuous place in the procession. Those entrusted with the command of divisions presently, by preconcerted signals, ranged their men into three portions, and soon after Lord George's arrival on the scene the word of command was given to march. Unfettered by anything but optional obedience to temporary and amateur authority, and thrilling with the burning fanaticism that had been kindled and quickened by their leader in his mad and incendiary speeches—a leader both morally and physically unfitted for the awful responsibility that from henceforth rested on his feeble shoulders—the living mass set out on their march to Westminster. Each of the three portions took a different route, and crossed the river by a different bridge—one by Blackfriars, the second by Westminster, and the third, preceded by Lord George in his coach, by London Bridge, that portion being three miles in extent.

The whole multitude seems to have marched in perfect order and decorum—the three rivers of human beings flowing into every approach and avenue leading to the Houses of Parliament. Its arrival was proclaimed by an unanimous shout, described as being of such tremendous and terrible volume and portent as to fill the minds of all peaceable persons with dismay and alarm. It was about half-past two, and the members of Parliament began shortly after to arrive for the transaction of business. The Petition had been taken in and laid in the lobby of the House, into which place the crowd had penetrated, and but for the prompt closing of the door they would have flowed into the Chamber itself. The arrival of some of the Peers, who were about to assemble in their own Chamber, was the signal for the first breach of the peace. Blue banners waved from the tops of many of the adjacent houses as signals to the people which coaches they should attack. The first victim to their fury was the Archbishop of Canterbury. His coach was stopped and himself compelled to alight. They saluted him with groans and hisses, forcing him to cry 'No Popery,' which he is described as having done in a feeble voice. The Lord President of the Council—Earl Bathurst—an old and decrepit man, was dragged from his carriage and cruelly kicked, and it was with difficulty that he found refuge in the House.

The Bishop of Lincoln's coach was next stopped, and, showing some symptoms of resenting the indignities offered him, he was dragged out, and a ruffian seized him by the throat till blood came from his mouth. He managed to get to a gentleman's house, and escaped over the roof, while twenty or thirty of the mob were seeking for him below. Lord Mansfield—who was after to sit in judgment upon the author and abettor of all these outrages—was abused

and insulted, and mud was thrown in his face. The
Duke of Northumberland, the Bishop of Lichfield,
Lords Willoughby de Broke, Townshend, Hillsborough and many others were no less ill-used, and
their coaches all demolished. With every insult the
rabble became more and more outrageous, following
the Lords to the door of their House, which, however,
had been fortunately barred. Such were only a few
of the shameful assaults upon the Peers. The
members of the House of Commons escaped with
less damage, only two having been seriously attacked;
but the presence of the miscreants in the lobby was
a circumstance that added seriously to the threatening state of matters. Mr Ellis, one of the attacked
members, was pursued, and narrowly escaped assas-
sination; and the mob pressed so violently against
the door that divided them from the Chamber, that
every moment it seemed imminent that it would
break down and that the rabble would flood the
House.

Meantime Lord George Gordon had presented the
Petition, which was signed by 120,000 persons, and
moved to have it brought up, Alderman Bull second-
ing the motion. This was granted. Lord George
then asked to have it taken into immediate consideration; and being told that the rules of the
House did not permit it, he proceeded to divide the
House, when six Ayes voted against 192 Noes.
While this was proceeding he was repeatedly called
on by members to make an effort to disperse the

mob; but so far from complying with their requests he kept running backwards and forwards from his place in the House—to the window—to the staircase on the lobby—frequently addressing the multitude from one or the other, in language so far removed from conciliatory that he announced the name of each member that spoke against the cause, exciting the already half-frantic people to a further pitch of fury. He denounced Burke as one of their chief enemies, he threatened Lord North, and exhorted his hearers to 'continue steadfast to their glorious cause.' He promised himself to persevere, 'though there was little to be hoped from the House of Commons.' The confusion and noise were bewildering. Members came out in the vain hope of appealing successfully to the mob, but it was impossible to hear anything but the clamour and hubbub of the rabble. Lord George's name was described by a witness as being constantly 'chimed' by the crowd, while others pressed into the lobby shouting 'Repeal, repeal, repeal.'

While Lord George was in the midst of haranguing the people Colonel Murray, General Conway, and Colonel Holroyd advanced to remonstrate with him, telling him he was a disgrace to his family, and that Bedlam only was a fitting place for such conduct; while Conway warned him that should the rabble break into the Chamber, 'not into the heart of the first man that enters, but into yours I will plunge my sword.'

'See,' said Lord George to his howling followers—

'see how they strive to oppose the triumph of your cause.'

There was a moment, Conway told Horace Walpole, when it seemed imminent that Members would be compelled to open the doors and fight their way through the mob sword in hand.

The Assistant-Chaplain of the house, who seems to have kept his head better than many others, discovered Lord George at one moment, overcome with heat, fatigue and excitement, in the dining-room, where he had thrown himself on a chair and was seemingly half asleep. Addressing him peremptorily, the Chaplain told him that he himself had heard men in the crowd assert that they would disperse if Lord George told them it was desirable they should do so. He assured him he was convinced that all depended on the attitude he would assume. Lord George preserved an absolute silence; and leaving the room, once more addressed the people in more inflammatory language than ever, instancing the success of the Scotch people in their object by resolution and riot. Taking hold of the Chaplain's gown—he having followed him in the vain hope of controlling his mad folly—'See,' said he, 'this is the Chaplain of this House. Ask him *his* opinion of the Popish Bill!' Justly indignant at this cowardly attempt to turn the people's wrath upon him, the Chaplain told him angrily that every disastrous consequence would rest on his head. One of the mob then asked him if they should leave the lobby. He told them to use their own judgment, and do what they saw fit for their own cause.

A hot discussion was, during this scene of confusion, proceeding in the House of Lords. By the timely and judicious exertions of Sir Francis Molyneux, the incursion of the mob had been prevented. The Duke of Richmond, Lord Shelburne and many others animadverted in the severest terms upon the supineness of the Government, who, said Lord Shelburne, 'had been warned of the threatened storm, and had yet taken no precautions to prevent disturbance.' And while the full force of the Peers' denunciations was proceeding, Lord Boston, fresh from the hands of the sovereign people—his clothes in tatters, his bag gone, his face bleeding—entered the House, and for a short time all attention was centred in his plight. The discussion was, however, shortly resumed when Lord Hillsborough, a member of the Government, angrily asserted that notice *had* been given to the civil powers, and certain magistrates had received instructions ; the truth, Horace Walpole solemnly asserts, being that the Cabinet Council of the preceding day (Thursday) authorised Lord North to prepare the civil officers to take measures to keep the peace, and that he (Lord North) *forgot to do so* till two o'clock of the next day—that same day—when the procession had nearly arrived at Westminster.

The two magistrates who represented the civil powers were indicated as being present, and were questioned, and denied receiving any instructions

whatever.   In short, it was the old story, and everyone implicated tried to lay the blame on each other.
But meanwhile the foe was actually, as well as meta-
phorically at the gates—the danger was very imminent—and these scenes were but the prologue to the
drama, or rather to the tragedy, that followed.   A
written order was hastily delivered to the justices, em-
powering them to take means to disperse the rabble,
and the House adjourned.   The concourse of people
did not disperse till between nine and ten, when a detachment of Life Guards arrived and scattered them
with but little difficulty.

Never before in any reign or under any circumstances had so alarming and humiliating a spectacle
been witnessed in the realm—Lords and Commons
imprisoned in their own palace, bereft of power, authority, and dignity, by a furious and irresponsible
mob ; the town given up to the tender mercies of a
ruffianly and degraded rabble, who, by the success of
each fresh outrage gained renewed confidence in their
own power, and less control over their own passions.
Quitting the neighbourhood of Westminster, and
dividing themselves as in the morning, one portion
proceeded to the Sardinian Embassy in Duke Street,
Lincoln's Inn, where they pulled down the altar and
destroyed the contents of the chapel, while the other
portion did the same to the Bavarian Embassy.   Two
silver lamps were stolen from the former, and when
the engines arrived to quench the fire that had been
kindled to destroy the edifice, the people prevented

their being used, until a company of Foot Guards arrived, that had been fetched by a gentleman—a Mr Bearcroft—from Somerset Street Barracks. Colonel Wynyard, the commanding-officer, caused all persons found inside the chapel to be arrested, and, forming his men round three deep, made a prison of the street.

Thirteen were arrested and taken to the Savoy, and amongst them a Russian officer, who was liberated the next day, when they were all examined, some remanded, one discharged, and five sent to Newgate. Mr Bearcroft was duly warned that his house would be destroyed for the part he had taken. It was so, and all its contents burned in the streets. It seems incredible that, in the face of such alarming incidents, no effort should have been made by the authorities to suppress the ever-growing tumults, save by sending a handful of soldiers to some spot already infested by the rioters, and who irritated without subduing them. So it was, however. After pausing on Saturday they assembled on Sunday in Moorgate Street, and with the now established cry of 'No Popery' soon gathered together a large number of idlers and roughs, and attacking a Roman Catholic Chapel in Ropemaker's Walk demolished its contents. A company of Guards appearing, they decamped. No person up to now had been killed by the soldiery; and, probably encouraged by this fact, the mob reassembled on Monday and commenced burning, plundering, and destroying as they moved along, and gaining assurance at every step, vowed vengeance on all who opposed their pro-

gress. Some carried trophies of the pillages of
Friday and Sunday, and paraded before Lord George's
house, afterwards burning them in an adjacent field.
Again dividing themselves, one party went to Wap-
ping, another to Smithfield, and a third to Sir George
Savile's house, which they gutted, together with those
of two other gentlemen—Messrs Moberley and Rain-
forth—who had given evidence at the examination of
the thirteen arrested rioters.

The five who had been committed to Newgate had
been escorted there by a file of Guards, who were
pelted and stoned by the mob during the execution of
their duty. The soldiers behaved with the greatest
forbearance ; still, so much did the rabble fear them,
that each section of the mob stationed scouts to
watch all the approaches to the spot on which they
were operating, so that they might on the first alarm
of their proximity decamp. On this day—Monday—
a Proclamation was issued by the Government, offering a reward of £500 for the apprehension of those
concerned in the destruction of the Sardinan and
Bavarian Embassies ; and the Protestant Association
circulated a handbill requesting all true Protestants
to show their attachment to the cause by 'legal and
decent deportment,' while Lord George, not to be
behindhand, disseminated one on his own account,
disclaiming all complicity with the rioters, recommending peace and order, and promulgating the most
Christianlike injunctions for good behaviour. But the
arm of the law was paralysed, and no decided measures

were resorted to by the amazed and incapable Government.

The following day, Tuesday the 6th, was that upon which the Houses of Parliament were to meet again. All the military in the town were ordered on duty there and at the Tower; but in spite of these precautions Lord Sandwich's coach, which was conveying him to the House of Lords, was stopped on its way thither, himself assaulted, and severely wounded in the face. He was rescued with difficulty, and escorted by soldiers to his own residence.

Crowds again assembled before both Houses, and were fully as numerous and threatening as on the previous Friday. Seeming more orderly at first, they speedily became tumultuous, and it was deemed prudent to cause a detachment of Foot Guards to occupy Westminster Hall, the doors of which were then closed to prevent the mob from entering. Several of the Members, amongst whom was Burke, walked down to the House, and were surrounded by some of the more orderly and respectable of the malcontents who expostulated with them for supporting the obnoxious bill. Entering the House, Burke spoke with indignant fire and eloquence of the humiliating condition of public affairs—of the 'bludgeoned mob' awaiting them in the streets, while a military force with fixed bayonets had to guard them at their door.

Resolutions were passed, one being an assertion of Members privileges; a second voted for a committee

S

to inquire into the late and present outrages, and for the discovery of their authors and promoters ; a third for a prosecution by the Attorney-General ; and a fourth voted an address to the King for the reimbursement of the foreign Ministers to the amount of damage they had sustained by the riots. They agreed also to consider the petitions from many of His Majesty's Protestant subjects. The Lords met likewise, but the state of tumult, together with the fact that they had to be guarded by a military force and that the First Lord had been severely wounded by the rabble, decided them to adjourn, which they did, to the 19th. Intelligence of conflagrations in the City was also received by the House of Commons, and a hasty adjournment took place there also. Meantime, Lord George, in spite of his appeals in the cause of peace and goodwill before mentioned, had been in his place in the House wearing the blue cockade ostentatiously in his hat. One of the Members, Colonel Herbert, indignantly declared that if he did not at once remove the insignia of riot he would himself cross the House and compel him to do so. At this one or two of Lord George's supporters—there were but six in all—interfered, and he being unwilling to give it up, it was forced from him. During the discussion that ensued he once more attempted to leave the House to address the populace, but he was forcibly detained. Sir George Osborne went out and warned them that unless they dispersed, the militia had orders to fire upon them.

'We will repel force by force,' they replied.

Justice Hyde launched a body of cavalry amongst them, and he having besides this made himself obnoxious by helping to rescue Lord Sandwich from their hands, one Jackson, a sailor, hoisted a black and red flag, and heading the mob, marched to Lisle Street, where Mr Hyde's house was situated. A party of Guards was sent after them, but too late to avert the mischief. When the house had been destroyed, Jackson in a stentorian voice called out 'To Newgate, ahoy!' and once more placing himself at their head, led the rabble down Holborn to rescue their imprisoned comrades.

The principal keeper of the gaol, Mr Akerman, had been warned that they contemplated visiting the prison and liberating the prisoners; and he, being a resolute and fearless man, took every precaution that the emergency seemed to call for, and relying on the enormous strength of the walls and defences, probably believed that even if he and his companions chanced to fall into their hands and got roughly treated, at least the prison would be proof against their attacks. The sequel showed their error. Akerman bolted and barred every opening to his dwelling—which formed an outer part of the gaol—and awaited their arrival. By seven o'clock the street was filled with the horde of tramping miscreants, who were preceded by thirty men, walking three abreast, each carrying a crowbar, or a sledge hammer or a pickaxe, and all tools necessary to carry out their design, which tools had been sacked from shops on their march. The multitude

that followed had all the appearance of being perfectly
organised.   One of them, clearly acting from preconcerted instructions, knocked at Mr Akerman's door;
no one replying to the summons he ran down the
steps of the house, bowed to the crowd, pointed
significantly to the door and retired.

Akerman appeared at a window and shouted his
refusal either to yield up his charges or to surrender
the place.   He then escaped through the gaol and
made his way to the sheriffs, to seek the assistance
of the magistrates, who still hung back.   The Lord
Mayor, one Brackley Kenneth, proved himself utterly
inefficient and cowardly in the emergency—unable to
grapple with a difficulty—which, however, had proved
an equally tough one to more spirited and intelligent
men than he.

The crowd now deliberately divided itself: one part
attacked Akerman's dwelling, the second went to the
felons' door, and the third to the debtors'.   Bludgeons
quickly demolished Akerman's windows, and a 'mad
Quaker,' the son of a rich corn factor, wearing a
mariner's jacket, drove a scaffold pole like a battering-
ram through the shutters.   Mounting on his shoulders,
a lad rammed in the broken shutter with his own head.
A chimney-sweep was the first in, and was wildly
cheered by the mob.   He was closely followed by the
Quaker, who directly after appeared at the first-floor
window.   The door was forced open and all the contents of the house pitched out, a heap made, and set
on fire.   It is a curious instance of the way that the

wild fire of contagion had run through the whole town, that all this time there were standing round, a circle of well-dressed men, who encouraged the rioters by every means in their power.

Many of the actors in this special scene appeared to have lost all control over their actions, and literally and actually to have gone mad. One Sims, a tripe man, rushing up to the great gate of the Old Bailey— a ponderous and apparently impregnable tower of strength—swore desperately that it should fall. From this moment there was no pause in the people's fury. Like demons suddenly let loose they rushed upon the gate with sledge-hammers and pickaxes, hurling their combined strength and fury upon it to demolish the stubborn and apparently immovable barrier. Many belonging to the more respectable classes—shopmen, servants—seemed to catch the horrid infection, and added blow to blow to demolish they hardly knew what, with a fury whose cause it was not possible to trace.

Now it was that the Gordon riots reached their climax, and continued at high-water mark until the followed Thursday. Several times the gates caught fire, and as many did the turnkeys who stood the siege inside push down with broomsticks the burning furniture which had been piled there by the mob, and swill them with water to keep the lead from melting that soldered the hinges. It was all in vain; the flames had now well-nigh demolished that part of the prison that was inhabited by Akerman, and had spread to the lodge, then to the chapel, and one after the other

to the different wards.   The horrors of the scene were
increased by the terror of the unhappy prisoners, who,
all manacled and fettered, believed that they must be
burnt to death.   Their cries and oaths mingled with
the rabble's, whose efforts to get at them became more
and more desperate.   The supreme moment arrived—
the ponderous gate at length yielded—and the whole
mass of people flooded the gaol.   The prisoners rushed
to and fro, beating the walls and bars; while the glare
of the fire and the confusion and din exceeded in horror
all that could be imagined or described in Dante's
'Hell.'   But, like the gate, the bars yielded, the walls
were partially demolished ; and amid yells, cheers, and
screams, three hundred prisoners stood released from
their incarceration.   Some were dragged out by their
liberators senseless and bleeding, some were conducted
away by their friends in the crowd, and some were seen
lifted by their sympathisers on to horses, encumbered
with their fetters and shackles.   The engines, at their
best of little more use than tea-kettles, arrived.   The
fire raged, the mob yelled and whooped ; and that no
incident should be wanting in the dramatic effect, an
opening was made in the crowd, and there, in a coach
drawn by some of his bludgeoners, appeared Lord
George Gordon, bowing complacently to the populace.

Years later, when it was resolved upon to drain the
lake that occupied the present site of the gardens in
St James' Square, the keys of Newgate were discovered lying at the bottom, where they had pre-

sumably been flung by some guilty and terrified rioter after the tumults had subsided.

That same night, Tuesday, 6th, while these scenes were proceeding at Newgate, another mob had attacked Lord Mansfield's house in Bloomsbury Square. They forced their way into his magnificent mansion, which contained not only beautiful pictures and works of art, but an invaluable library, and a treasure store of rare MSS. These were all pitched out of the windows and destroyed—women and children assisting in the wholesale annihilation. Lord and Lady Mansfield escaped by the back door, or they would in all probability have fallen victims to the insensate fury of the mob. A file of foot soldiers arrived, drew up near the blazing pile which had been made of these effects, but appear to have taken little heed to the rioters. Some Life Guards arrived, and then the mob was fired on and six people killed. With banners flying and triumphant shouts and yells they took their way to Caen Wood, Lord Mansfield's residence at Hampstead; but finding it protected by the soldiery, they made no serious attempts upon it. Another portion proceeded from Bloomsbury to Mr Langdale's, a Roman Catholic distiller in Holborn.

An enormous concourse of people assembled here, attacked the buildings, and fired them. They seized the vats and barrels containing the spirits manufactured there, and emptied all their contents at hazard Hundreds drank themselves into insensibility, and not a few to death. Some—too intoxicated to lift themselves up from where they fell—were trampled to death. Others perished in the flames. More met their deaths during this episode than were otherwise killed during the whole of the six days' riots. The gutters ran with gin, brandy, and spirits of all kinds, and the people—men, women, and children—lay themselves down to imbibe the fiery liquid.

On this day an attack had been made on the Bank —an attempt which was repulsed by John Wilkes and the soldiers on guard. The anxiety and fears of the Government seem to have been roused by this incident, which, however, had been threatened for some time. The metropolis, so long absolutely at the mercy of the lawless ruffians, now saw a prospect of deliverance.

The rabble, emboldened by the impunity with which their criminal acts had been treated, had sent notice of their approach to the officers of the public buildings and messages to Wedderburn, Lords Stormont, Ashburnham, and several others of the Ministry, warning them of their intentions. The houses of the Ministers, however, were now protected by the military, and wherever this proved to be the case the mob considered discretion to be the better part of valour. They had announced their intention of visiting the Fleet Prison on the Tuesday night, and of freeing the prisoners ; and it is amongst the curious facts of this happily, hitherto, unique episode of London's history that these unfortunate prisoners begged piteously that they might not be rescued at

night, as many of the poor creatures had no other
asylum than the sheltering roof of their miserable
gaol. Thus it happened that it was on Wednesday
that the burning of the Fleet Prison and the liberation
of its inmates were effected. Horace Walpole asserts
that but little excitement prevailed in the fashionable
quarters of London, and that the amusements there
proceeded without check, though there were passages
in his letters written at the time that points to this
allegation as being at all events an exaggerated one.
It would indeed be difficult to describe the alarm and
dismay that pervaded the greater part of the town.
A wild rumour was disseminated, and found credence
with many, that the rioters contemplated opening the
doors of Bedlam and releasing the maniacs incarcerated there, and that they were about to liberate the
wild beasts that were then enchained in the Tower.

It was said that the King had been kidnapped—
murdered—that the palace was burned—and a thousand reports of all sorts were circulated, none of which
were impossible, or even unlikely, in the existing state
of things. Seventy two private houses, four gaols,
and property to the amount of £180,000 were destroyed. Later on compensation from the public
purse, in pursuance of a vote in the House of
Commons, was awarded to those who had suffered.
The sum was levied upon various wards in the
City, and upon the Southwark and county boroughs.
Lord Mansfield and Sir George Savile refused all
indemnification.

We have up to this time (Wednesday) concerned ourselves entirely with the doings of the mob and the Parliament. Let us now examine a little the proceedings of the King and the Council. Of all the statesmen upon whom lay the enormous weight of responsibility involved in the preservation of the public safety, the King alone stood firm and undaunted at this critical juncture. Although the timidity and pusillanimity of those who were bound to assist him with their counsel and support filled him with anxiety and distress of mind, he did not shrink from the duty thus unfairly laid upon him. But for his resolution and firmness it is probable that the disgraceful scenes that had been enacted without check or hindrance for five days would have continued still longer ; it is even possible that a large portion of the capital would have been destroyed.

The King convened a meeting of the Privy Council for this day (Wednesday), at which he presided. There were two questions upon which he and his Ministers were at variance : first, what amount of ill-behaviour on the part of the rioters could warrant a magistrate in giving an order to the military to fire on the mob; and second, whether previous to giving such order it was imperative that the Riot Act should be read. On this point the Ministry were divided, and would probably have remained divided, but for the resolute action of the Monarch. Lord Bathurst, the President of the Council, and Sir Fletcher Norton, the Speaker, supported his views, while all the other Ministers insisted that not only should the Act be read, but that an hour must intervene between its reading and the order to fire. Indignant at this hesitation and cowardice, George III. announced his intention of acting upon his own responsibility should his Ministers refuse to support him. He was fully alive to the odium that would almost certainly attach itself to him should he alone authorise the severe measures he knew were imperative, but the King possessed the courage of his opinions as well as the dignity of his order. He announced that as his Council refused him their assistance, he would act without it. He would, he said, mount his horse, head his Guards in person and disperse the rioters.

'There shall be *one*,' he said, with emphasis and emotion—'*one* I can answer for, that will do his duty.'

It was the sixth day of the riots, and the danger was still growing. At the moment that the Council was breaking up, Wedderburn, afterwards Lord Loughborough, and then the King's Attorney-General, appeared upon the scene. The King at once addressed him, and putting the facts concisely before him, charged him to answer in his character of Attorney-General. Wedderburn promptly and positively endorsed the Sovereign's opinion; and thus fortified, the Privy Councillors reluctantly assented to an Order in Council being sent to Lord Amherst, the Commander-in-Chief, at once to disperse the rioters without any further warrant from the civil

powers. Later, Lord Mansfield, the most eminent
lawyer of the day, supported these views in a powerful and eloquent speech in the House of Lords.

A camp of 10,000 men was formed in Hyde Park
on the night of Wednesday, ten militia regiments
being summoned to aid nine regiments of regulars.
All the militia regiments but two were encamped in
Hyde Park and in St James' Park and in the gardens of Montagu House, now the British Museum.
To this significant menace the miscreants at once
succumbed, and in twenty-four hours the town, which
in many parts bore the appearance of having stood
a siege, became quiet, the mob betook themselves to
their refuges, and people began to breathe more freely.
The fact may not be without interest to the cynical
that John Wilkes on this ocassion prominently
espoused the cause of law and order. His diary
exists in the British Museum, detailing his services.
At the head of a band of armed citizens he defended
an attack on Blackfriars Bridge, upon which, since
1766, an unpopular toll of one halfpenny had been
levied on foot passengers ; and in consequence of this
the toll-house was marked for destruction, and was,
together with bar, books, and accounts burned. Several men were thrown into the river during the
encounter. The 'Wilkes and Liberty' tumults that
had taken place twelve years prior to Lord George
Gordon's efforts in the same direction had apparently
assuaged the thirst of that so-called patriot for riots
and sedition ; or, at all events—and this sufficient for

our purpose—of such riots of which he was not himself the hero and apotheosis. John Wilkes, in short,
had ceased for some years to be a rebellious 'patriot,'
and had blossomed into a law-abiding Alderman, having filled first the posts of Alderman and Sheriff; in
1774 the not unremumerative office of Lord Mayor, and
finally in 1779 the extremely lucrative one of Cham-
berlain of the City of London. He helped to disperse a mob in Fleet Street and did duty on the night of
Lord George's arrest in St Sepulchre's Churchyard.

The following is said to be a true copy of the return
made to Lord Amherst of those who were killed and
wounded during the six days' tumults :—

By light horse	101
By troops and guards	109
Died in hospitals	75
Prisoners under care . . .	173
Total	458

To these must be added those who perished by
accident, those who drank themselves to death at
Langdale's distillery, and those who expiated their
crimes on the gallows.

On the 9th another meeting of the Privy Council was
held, and a warrant issued for Lord George Gordon's
arrest. The messengers charged with the execution
of this duty repaired to his house, gained easy admis-
sion, and informing him of their business ; he at once
entered a hackney coach and was driven to the Horse
Guards. A squadron of light horse were stationed
in the adjoining street in case of resistance. A long

examination before the Secretaries of State and other members of the Privy Council ensued, and Lord George was finally despatched to the Tower, his coach surrounded by far the greatest number of Guards that had ever before escorted a prisoner of State. On this same day Mr Fisher, the Secretary of the Protestant Association, was arrested and examined, but he was liberated.

On the 19th there was a debate in the House of Commons, when Fox, while supporting the address to the Throne, which was one of thanks for the measures taken by the King for the restoration of public order, severely blamed the inaction of the Government. Burke also declaimed vehemently against the rioters, and lauded the Relief Bill which they desired to repeal. He also animadverted in forcible terms on those in power, asserting that the King's Bench Prison might have escaped destruction had attention been paid to certain information sent to the Commander-in-Chief; while the sensitive and scandalised Wilkes declared that had the Chief Magistrate done his duty much mischief would have been averted. In the House of Peers, Lord Mansfield bestowed the great weight of his approval and advocacy upon the measures taken by the King, basing his opinion upon his profound legal knowledge. The metropolis, he declared, would have been burned but for the Sovereign's decisive action ; and the assistance of the military was not only timely, but strictly in accordance with the law. The soldiers, he said, whether wearing red coats or brown, had acted as citizens.

On the 28th June, 1785, rioters were tried at the Old Bailey. Thirty-five were capitally convicted, and forty-three were acquitted. One woman—a negress —was executed, and another woman was sentenced to be whipped for stealing a pewter cup. Seventeen of the condemned rioters were respited, and eighteen were hanged.

The correspondence, if that word is not a misnomer, when the written communication is all on one side which passed between Lord Stormont, one of the Secretaries of State, and the Lord Mayor during the progress of the riots was published, but it did not redound to the credit of either. Lord Stormont urgently exhorted the First Magistrate to take drastic measures for the repression of the tumults, but by carefully avoiding, however, to indicate in words the nature of the course thus ambiguously recommended, he contrived to elude any responsibility that might follow on his advice being taken. The Lord Mayor, however, proved equal to the occasion, and took the simple and effectual method of not answering the letters ; and when urged on this point assured Lord Stormont—by message, and with a vagueness that rivalled Lord Stormont's—that 'he would use his best endeavours to this end.' For some unexplained reason—possibly in order that popular feeling might have time to calm down—Lord George's trial did not take place for eight months after these events. During this time the stringent and severe rules that had been at first laid down for his safe keeping were very much relaxed, and he was permitted many indulgences.

On the day appointed for trial he was conveyed from the Tower to the Court of King's Bench. The streets were filled with spectators, and coaches lined the highway. Attired in a suit of black velvet he entered the Hall with a firm air and a not undignified deportment. When the jury were challenged he objected smilingly to a ropemaker, because, he said, ' he was interested professionally in the result.'

The indictment was a long one. He was charged with levying war against the King's Majesty . . . to effect by force an alteration in the law of the country. This, of course, involved high treason. The Judge was the Lord Chief Justice—Lord Mansfield—himself one of the greatest sufferers from the actions of the prisoner. Council for the Crown were the Attorney-General and the Solicitor-General, while the Hon. Thomas Erskine and Mr Kenyon defended Lord George. The trial lasted from eight o'clock a.m. on Monday to five p.m. on Tuesday. Many witnesses were called for the Crown, and the evidence given by them was to all appearance conclusive and incontrovertible.

All the genius and eloquence of Mr Erskine—a young lawyer whose right to distinction was first achieved on this occasion—were brought to bear upon the defence of his unworthy client, whose indisputable guilt was doubtless but one more incentive to exertion to extricate him from his emergency; and added another laurel to the young orator's wreath of victory. In the excitement of the moment he permitted himself to overstep the limits prescribed by usage to prisoners' counsel, and called God to witness the innocence of his client's actions. 'He who could blame such honest and artless conduct is a ruffian,' he concluded.   We believe that only once since, has any eminent counsel indulged in such an irregularity. This was in the case of the murder of Lord William Russell, when Charles Phillips called God to witness the innocence of Courvoisier.*

The Lord Chief-Justice summed up and addressed the jury.

It cannot be sufficiently impressed upon the mind of Englishmen, proud of qualities of the great men of their country, that, flinging aside all feeling of personal resentment and sense of injury, Lord Mansfield, if he erred at all in his dignified and admirable charge, erred on the side of mercy.

With a lofty wisdom he explained the law, and while denying that Sir G. Savile's Bill encouraged Popery, he affirmed it to be an erroneous religion and one that should be restrained.   Judges are, no doubt bound to act impartially; but this was an instance where stern severity would have seemed almost inevitable.   He summed up a clear, enlightened and moderate speech by stating that the case depended

* Mr Erskine became Lord Chancellor in 1806.

on two points : one was whether the multitude
assembled and committed deeds of violence with
intent to terrify the Legislature into compliance with
their desire that the Act be repealed.   If their opinion
were in the negative, the prisoner should be acquitted.
The other was : Did the prisoner incite the insurrection, intending to enforce a repeal of the law ?   He
stated that he purposely avoided making observations,
leaving them to form their own opinion; and if they
were not fully satisfied of his guilt on this point they
were to acquit him.   The jury retired, and returning into Court after half an hour's deliberation, pronounced the verdict of Not Guilty.

The Protestant Association was jubilant, and wrote
Lord George fulsome and congratulatory laudations,
teeming with texts, ascribing the glory of his acquittal
to Divine interposition, and charging him 'to walk
before God in the land of the living.'   The riots, the
Association asserted, were begun by the Papists in
order to injure the sacred cause ; and it pointed out
that not one Protestant petitioner out of the 44,000
was 'either apprehended, tried, convicted, executed,
or killed,' whilst in everyone of these predicaments
Papists were to be found.   Lord George responded in
the same key, calling God to witness that he had had
no part in the tumults.

Entirely unabashed by the estimation in which he
was held by all reasonable and reputable persons, he
continued to keep himself before the public.   Every
effort was made by his brother the Duke of Gordon

and other relatives to induce him to retire into private life, but in vain. He was resolved to quaff the bowl of notoriety to the dregs. Immediately after his acquittal he tried to obtain audience of the King, and failing in this, he applied for the same favour to the Prince of Wales, but here also he was refused. In 1782 he visited Paris, and was there presented to Marie Antoinette. During his stay he formed a friendship with the impostor Cagliostro, in whose wiles and arts he became involved, Cagliostro being one of the causes of his ultimate incarceration in Newgate.

Soon after his return he protested against the restoration of their forfeited estates to the rebels of 1745. There seems to have been no public question upon which he hesitated to exhort, counsel, and instruct. He tormented Pitt with letters containing his crude and foolish views on taxation ; he got up a demonstration against the shop-tax ; he intrigued with the Dutch ambassador, and endeavoured to entice British seamen to enter the Dutch service (Holland at that moment was watching her opportunity to declare in favour of American Independence against England) ; he entered into correspondence with Mr Pitt, enclosing him addresses that he said he had received from British sailors desiring to serve the Protestant interests in Holland. Not receiving a prompt reply to this communication he wrote again, stating he considered Mr Pitt 'very rude' for not replying sooner. He sent memorials to all the different statesmen of Europe, acquainting them with the purposes and intentions of

the ' Protestant Association.' In connection with the
Dutch affair a crowd of deluded sailors went to Buckingham House clamouring for employment ; and finding no redress, a feeling of anger grew up against Lord
George, and they adjourned to his house, vowing
vengeance against him. The rumour of their approach had gone before them, and the neighbourhood
was terrified. They knocked at the door, and he (to
do him justice, he was no coward) opened it in person,
and, addressing them in one of his long-winded
speeches, laid the blame on the Ministers, and assured
them that he was their friend and advocate. In one
moment the temper of the mob was changed, and
their anger diverted in another channel. The air,
which but a few minutes before had resounded with
furious objurgations directed against Lord George, was
now rent with the cry of 'Gordon and Liberty,' and
many inquired whether they should not go and pull
down Pitt's house. This question Lord George answered *with a low bow*, and doubtless he regretted the
rabble did not carry their suggestion into execution.

In 1786 he was excommunicated by the Archbishop
of Canterbury for refusing to give evidence in the
Ecclesiastical Court concerning the will of a clergy-
man at whose death he had been present ; his deposi-
tion being necessary. The punishment did not affect
him very seriously, and he made the pertinent (and
impertinent) observation that to ' expel him from a
society to which he did not belong was an absurdity
worthy of an Archbishop.'

His attachment to Protestantism, the peg which he
had hitherto used whereupon to hang his notoriety,
appears about this time (1786) to have begun to yield
to the superior attractions of Judaism. Not Protestantism alone, but Christianity lost favour in his eyes ;
and in due course he embraced that faith. The Jews
welcomed him ' as a second Moses.' He conformed
to all the ceremonies of the ancient fathers, and expected all who professed the same religion to do
likewise.

In April 1787, informations were exhibited against
him in the Court of King's Bench, one at the suit of
the Attorney-General, for a libel entitled ' The
Prisoners' Petition,' purporting to come from the
prisoners in Newgate, reflecting on the administration
of justice there and in the country ; and the other at
the suit of the French ambassador, for a libellous and
injurious publication against the Queen of France.
He refused to employ counsel for his defence on the
score of poverty, arguing with the Court and bringing forward every sort of factitious opposition and
quibble to postpone the issue. Time after time the
Court adjourned, and it was not till June 6 that the
trial commenced.

There was no moral doubt whatever that this tirade
of treason, blasphemy and folly was his own production, though purporting to emanate from the prisoners.
Imputations on the Sovereign, and wearisome and
blasphemous extracts from the Old Testament, were
among its salient features. Mr Erskine, his success-

ful champion at his first trial, was now, together with
the Attorney-General, arrayed against him.

He was found guilty of both charges. His speech
on the last was so violent and indecorous that he was
stopped in its delivery, and the Attorney-General
declared indignantly that he was unworthy of the
name of Briton ; yet, for some unexplained reason, he
was permitted to withdraw at the end of the trial
before sentence was pronounced, and without bail.
Taking advantage of the opportunity thus, surely
intentionally, afforded to him, he escaped to Holland.
Shortly after his arrival in Amsterdam the burgo-
masters peremptorily commanded him to leave the
city within the space of twenty-four hours. Leaving
Holland he returned to England, and landed at
Harwich in July. From thence he proceeded to
Birmingham, where he lived in hiding until December.
Here he consorted entirely with Jews, adopting their
dress and manners. On the 7th December he was
apprehended and taken to London, and immediately
brought up to the Court of King's Bench to receive
his sentence. In delivering judgment, Judge Ashurst
told him that the document called 'The Prisoners'
Petition' was fictitious and of his own fabrication,
written by him manifestly to excite insurrection and
sedition and discontent amongst the prisoners ; and
that as to the crime of which he had also been found
guilty—that of aspersing the character of the Queen
of France—it would be doing him too much honour
to read these libels, so full of scurrilous language and

low abuse. He regretted that one descended from
such illustrious ancestors should thus have dishonoured
his family. For the offence of publishing the 'Petition'
he was sentenced to be imprisoned in Newgate for three
years. For the libel he was fined £500, and further
imprisoned for two years after the expiration of the
first judgment. He was also to give security for
fourteen years' good behaviour—himself in £10,000,
and sureties in £2000 each. Attired in Jewish garb,
and decked with a long and flowing beard, Lord
George bowed in ostentatious humility to the finding
of the Court. The extraordinary clemency with which
he was treated was continued up to the last, for the
royal pardon was soon after offered him, provisionally,
if he recanted his opinions, and promised to lead a
quiet life for the future. He replied 'that to sue for
pardon was a confession of guilt, and that his public
conduct should never disgrace the principles he had
espoused, and that the tender mercies of the wicked
were cruelties.'

Thus, in Newgate he remained—manifestly by his
own choice. He bore his confinement with equanimity, and was treated with the greatest consideration
by the authorities—of course in accordance with their
instructions. He enjoyed good health, had regular
diet, rose at eight, and went to bed at eleven; read
the papers, wrote letters, and received visitors at
twelve; played the violin, and had six or seven guests
to dinner every day. He enjoyed concerts of music
and had dancing parties. He fasted according to the

rites of the Jewish Church, was kind and considerate to his fellow-prisoners, doing all in his power to alleviate their distress. From hence he forwarded a memorial to the 'friends of liberty,' inveighing against all power but that of democracy.

In 1789 the news of the capture of the Bastille, which took place on the 14th July of that year, penetrated even into the interior of Newgate, where in all probability the occupants believed a similar day of deliverance might dawn for them. Suffering as he was in part for the attack on the Queen of France, Lord George prepared and despatched a petition to the National Assembly of France, putting forth that he was imprisoned for his attempt to succour the oppressed there. He therefore prayed them to apply to the Court of St James for the remission of his sentence. The Abbé Gregoire replied on behalf of the Assembly that as Lord George was a foreigner and was detained in an English prison, it would be highly improper for the Assembly to deliberate 'à son égard,' and recommended him to apply to the English Tribunal. Lord George replied by indignantly inquiring of the National Assembly whether under the new régime the powers of France were curtailed, and whether the French ambassador at the English Court would refuse to obey their commands if these were laid upon him to demand his release? Once more he passionately claimed their interference, and inquired—not without some show of reason— whether now that they themselves slept in safety

from the cruel dungeons of the Bastille they could
without emotion suffer him to be incarcerated with
murderers and thieves, and make no effort on his
behalf! He concluded his invocation by the extraordinary argument that he was brother to a man of
the birth and importance of the Duke of Gordon.

On the 28th January 1793, his term of imprison-
ment having expired, he once more appeared in the
Court of King's Bench. Enormous crowds assembled
to see him. He entered with his hat on, and being
desired by the judge to remove it, he did so, and
proceeded to bind his head round with a handkerchief
of three colours in the form of a turban. He asked
permission to address the Court, which was accorded
him. He then said he was ready to pay the fine of
£500, and asserted he was able to find the necessary
securities, mentioning two of his friends, whose means
however proved to be insufficient. He was again
remanded to Newgate, and as he was being removed
he observed with an angry frown that he 'felt more
for the servile complaisance of the Court than for his
own misfortunes.' But he was not designed to drag
out his wearisome and profitless existence much
longer. Gaol fever—more or less always then present
in Newgate—struck him down in December. On the
eighth day of his illness he was informed of the death
of the unhappy Marie Antionette, when he observed
that she was 'not the last member of the Royal
Family of France that would perish by the guillotine.'

Shortly afterwards he became delirious, repeatedly

calling his brother and addressing him as if he were present, and muttering sentences by which he had in former days rallied round him his fanatical and vagabond followers and filled them with the spirit of rebellion and riot. Gaunt and emaciated he lay upon his prison bed, helpless, unconscious, and forsaken of his own; his shattered life the grievous result of his lawless and seditious career. With a last effort he raised himself in his bed, and half chanted, half spoke the opening words of the republican song 'Ça ira'— words that at that time were infecting half Christendom. With this expiring tribute to an evil cause, his spirit passed away.

Lord George Gordon has, I think, been erroneously pronounced mad by posterity. To me he seems to have been only extravagantly vain. Throughout all the wild and turbulent scenes that he first recklessly provoked and then deliberately encouraged, there was no occasion when he lost either his powers of acting rationally and consistently with a view to the success of his designs, nor did he lose his self-control under circumstances that might well try the nerves of the strongest. His intentions and deeds were criminal, and all his actions are consistent with this theory.

THE END.

CPSIA information can be obtained
at www.ICGtesting.com
Printed in the USA
LVHW080040150120
643609LV00018B/464